C

CLASSIC
FILM
SCRIPTS

BLOW-UP

a film by

Michelangelo Antonioni

Lorrimer Publishing

Published by Lorrimer Publishing Incorporated
First printing 1971
Revised edition 1984
Publisher and Editor: Andrew Sinclair

Antonioni, Michelangelo
  Blow up.
  I. Title
  791.43'72   PN1997

  ISBN 0-85647-096-1

Distributed exclusively in the United States of America,
its territories, possessions, protectorates, mandated territories,
the Philippines and Canada by Frederick
Ungar Publishing Company Incorporated,
36 Cooper Square, New York, N.Y. 10003

Distributed exclusively in the United Kingdom and
Commonwealth by Lorrimer (Sales) Limited.

Inquiries should be addressed to Lorrimer Publishing Limited,
16 Tite Street, London SW3 4HZ.

Cover design: Fred Price

CONTENTS

A NOTE ON THIS EDITION

This publication is based on the original screenplay of *Blow-Up*, and the dialogue cutting continuity of the final screen version. Antonioni has also produced an Italian-language edition of the script which contains his own special emphases and interpretations of the action. This script, translated by John Mathews, has also been used in the preparation of this publication, and all three sources have been combined to make as accurate a rendering as possible of the film which the British or American spectator will see on the screen. Technical description has been cut to a minimum to make for easier reading, but each change of shot is indicated by paragraphing for those who wish to make a closer analysis of the film. Certain scenes which appeared in the original screenplay were cut from the final version, and are indicated by numbers in the main text, which refer to footnotes collated at the end of the book. (See page 117.)

Acknowledgements and thanks are due to Metro-Goldwyn-Mayer Inc. for supplying the original screenplay and dialogue continuity, and also to Michelangelo Antonioni for the loan of his personal collection of production stills and for his general assistance in the preparation of this edition.

The translation of 'An Interview with Michelangelo Antonioni' by Pierre Billard is reproduced by kind permission of Grove Press Inc. The interview, which Antonioni answered in written form, was commissioned by Ulrich Gregor, and included in *Wie Sie Filmen*, edited by Ulrich Gregor, copyright © 1966 by Sigbert Mohn Verlag, Gütterslöh. 'Reality and *Cinéma Vérité*' by Michelangelo Antonioni has been translated from the article which appeared in the Latin-American edition of *Cinema Nuovo*, 1965. The extracts from 'Antonioni — English Style' have been translated from an article which appeared in *Cahiers du Cinéma* in January 1967. Finally, the extracts from the interview with Antonioni by Nadine Liber are reprinted by kind permission of *Life*, where they first appeared in January 1967.

AN INTERVIEW WITH MICHELANGELO ANTONIONI
by Pierre Billard

BILLARD : *In general, where does the original idea for your films come from?*

ANTONIONI : It seems to me that no one engaged in creative activity can answer that question in good faith. Lucidity is not one of my outstanding qualities. I look at everything, avidly, and I also think I listen a great deal.

One thing is certain : ideas come to me unexpectedly. But I'm not really interested in getting to the bottom of such a question.

B : *What does the writing of the scenario mean for you: clarifying the dramatic line, making the visual aspect of the film more specific, familiarizing yourself with the characters?*

A : To me, the visual aspect of a film is very closely related to its thematic aspect — in the sense that an idea almost always comes to me through images. The problem lies elsewhere. It has to do with restricting the accumulation of these images, with digging into them, with recognizing the ones that coincide with what interests me at the time.

It's work done instinctively, almost automatically, but it involves a great deal of tension. One's whole being is at stake : it is a precise moral choice.

What people ordinarily call the ' dramatic line ' doesn't interest me. One device is no better than another *a priori*. And I don't believe that the old laws of drama have validity any more. Today stories are what they are, with neither a beginning nor an end necessarily, without key scenes, without a dramatic arc, without catharsis. They can be made up of tatters, of fragments, as unbalanced as the lives we lead.

Familiarize myself with characters? But the characters are not strangers that I may or may not be on intimate terms with; they emerge out of me, they *are* my intimate inner life.

5

B : *What does the fact that you work in collaboration with others on your scenario mean to you?*

A : Every time I have tried to let others write parts of a rough script, the result, even if it was excellent from an objective point of view, was something foreign to me, something close to what I wanted without ever coinciding with it exactly. And that gave me a terrible sense of impotence. Then began the great task of selecting, correcting, even adapting, work that was as difficult as it was useless, because it inevitably led to compromise. I can never manage to be objective when I judge the work of my collaborators. The film stands between me and them. So, after trying this a few times, I ended up writing almost all the shooting scripts of my films myself.

However, I haven't ruled out collaborations altogether. I don't choose my collaborators on the basis of our affinities, but for the opposite reason. I need to have people who are very different from me around me, people with whom there can be animated, lively discussions. We talk, we discuss things for months before the film. We talk about a lot of things. Sometimes we also talk about the film, but not necessarily. What I say ricochets off them, comes back to me in the form of criticism, commentary, suggestions. After a certain time, the film becomes clear. It is only then that I begin to write the rough script. I work many hours a day, often beginning at dawn, until I'm completely exhausted.

B : *What form does your script take in its final phase?*

A : The shooting script is never definitive for me. It's notes about the direction, nothing more. There are no technical notations such as used to be made. The placing of the camera, the use of various lenses, the movements of the camera, all concern the phase in which the film is shot, not that in which the script is written.

I would say the same thing about dialogue. I have to hear the dialogue in the living voices of the actors, that is to say of the characters, within the scene, to decide whether or not it's right.

And then there's another factor. I believe in improvisation. None of us has the habit of preparing for a meeting to further business, love, or friendship; one takes these meetings as they come, adapting oneself little by little as they progress, taking advantage of unexpected things that come up. I experience the same things when I'm filming.

B : *Can the choice of locations or actors influence the scenario, and if so, how?*

A : In general, I decide upon the outdoor locations before writing the shooting script. In order to be able to write, I need to have the surroundings of the film clearly in mind. There are times too when an idea for a film comes to me from a particular place. Or more precisely, when certain locales come to mind because of the themes or characters running through my head. It's sometimes a rather odd series of coincidences.

B : *What possibilities for improvisation do you allow for while you're filming?*

A : Speaking of improvisation, I must add something to what I said before. If I think of the past, it's possible for me to say that I have always lived minute by minute. It's the way I live even today. Every moment of the day is important to me, every day is a new experience. And this doesn't change when I'm shooting. On the contrary, the pull of reality increases during shooting, because you're in an extremely receptive state, and because you're making new contacts, you're establishing often unexpected relationships with the crew, and these relationships are constantly changing. All that has a definite influence on my work, and leads me to improvised decisions, and even to radical changes. This is what I mean by improvisation . . .

B : *How are your relations with the crew?*

A : Excellent. I try to create a cordial atmosphere. I like to have people laughing and joking around me. People who seem to have no problems. It's quite enough that *I* have problems.

I admit, however, that I am very demanding. I don't allow anybody around me to show that he doesn't know his business. Or that he's unwilling to work. There is a certain laziness about crews, it's natural, inevitable. But it's what I dislike most. When I happen to scream at someone (as all directors do, it seems), I'm railing against this sort of indifference.

B : *What are your relations with the actors?*

A : I've always had excellent relations with actors — sometimes too good. Hearing me say that may seem odd, but it's true. Even with Jeanne Moreau, who claims the opposite, I have never — I repeat *never* — had arguments during filming.

I know, however, that actors feel somewhat uncomfortable with me; they have the feeling that they've been excluded from my work. And as a matter of fact they have been. But it is precisely this form of collaboration, and no other, that I ask of them.

Only one person has the film clearly in mind, insofar as that is possible: the director. Only one person fuses in his mind the various elements involved in a film, only one person is in a position to predict the result of this fusion : the director. The actor is one of these elements, and sometimes not even the most important. There is one thing the actor can't do, and that is to see himself in the view-finder; if he could, he'd come up with a number of suggestions regarding his acting. This privilege is reserved to the director, however, who will thus limit himself to manipulating ' the actor element ' according to criteria and exigencies known to him alone.

There are various ways of getting certain expressions from actors, and it is of no interest to know whether or not there is a corresponding mood behind these expressions.

I have often resorted to foreign actors for practical reasons : agreements with distributors, unavailability of Italian actors, and so forth. But sometimes it was because I thought actors were better suited to the roles than those at my disposal here.

B : *Do you prefer to record the sound on the set or to dub it afterwards?*

A : When I can, I prefer recording on the set. The sounds, the noises, and the natural voices as picked up by microphones have a power of suggestion that can't be obtained with dubbing. Moreover, most professional microphones are much more sensitive than the human ear, and a great many unexpected noises and sounds often enrich a sound track that's been made on the set.

Unfortunately, we are still not advanced enough technically to be able to use this system all the time. Shooting indoors, it's hard to get good sound. And dubbing also has its advantages. Sometimes I find that the transformation of a noise or of a sound becomes indispensable for certain special effects. Thus in certain cases it is necessary to change the human voice.

B: *Who decides on the exact framing and the camera movements?*
A: I can't imagine a director who would leave that up to other people. Excluding or including a detail, even an apparently secondary one, in the film image, choosing the angle of the shot, the lenses, the camera movements, are all decisions essential to the success of a film.

Technique is not something that can be applied from outside by just anybody. Practically speaking, technical problems don't exist. If style is there, it permeates technique. If style is missing, the problem disappears.

B: *Do you shoot any sequences from several angles so as to have greater freedom when you edit?*
A: Until *Red Desert*, I always filmed with a single camera, and thus from a single angle. But from *Red Desert* on, I began using several cameras with different lenses, but always from the same angle. I did so because the story demanded shots of a reality that had become abstract, of a subject that had become colour, and those shots had to be obtained with a long-focus lens.

Obviously I have the editing of the film clearly in mind during shooting. And it is only when I am led by circumstances to improvise, and consequently to shoot quickly, that I try to accumulate protection takes.

B: *How much do you have to do with the cutting of your films?*
A: I have always had an editor at my side on all my films. Except for *Cronaca di un Amore* this editor has been Eraldo da Roma. He is an extremely able technician with vast experience, and a man who loves his work. We cut the films together. I tell him what I want as clearly and precisely as possible, and he does the cutting. He knows me, he understands immediately, we have the same sense of proportion, the same sensibility concerning the duration of a shot.

B: *What is the role of music and the sound track in your films?*
A: I have always opposed the traditional musical commentary, the soporific function ordinarily assigned to it. It's this idea of ' setting images to music ', as if it were a question of an opera libretto, that

9

I don't like. What I reject is this refusal to let silence have its place, this need to fill supposed voids . . .

The only way to accept music in films is for it to disappear as an autonomous expression in order to assume its role as one element in a general sensorial impression. And with colour films today this is even more necessary.

B : *Do you concern yourself with the public and its possible reactions at any stage of making your films?*

A : I never think of the public. I think of the film. Obviously, you're always speaking to someone, but this partner in the conversation is always an ideal one (perhaps another self). If this weren't true, I wouldn't know what to base my work on, since there are at least as many publics as there are continents or human races — not to mention nations.

B : *What phase of making a film presents the most difficulty, requires the most effort?*

A : Each film has its own history. One will demand inhuman efforts during shooting, another intellectual tension at the scripting stage, another an iron will during the cutting or the dubbing, when you'd swear that the material you have on hand is completely different from what you wanted.

And then we each have our private lives which are not broken off during filming; on the contrary, they acquire new point and bite, giving our work a function that is sometimes stimulating, sometimes debilitating, sometimes calming, and so forth.

B : *Do you feel that the language of film has evolved, and to what extent do you think you have contributed to this evolution?*

A : My contribution to the formation of a new cinematic language is a matter that concerns critics. And not even today's critics, but rather those of tomorrow, if film endures as an art and if my films resist the ravages of time.

1965

REALITY AND *CINEMA-VERITE*

by Michelangelo Antonioni

The camera hidden behind a keyhole is a tell-tale eye which captures what it can. But what about the rest? What about what happens beyond the limits of its field of vision? It's not enough. So, make ten, a hundred, two hundred holes, install as many cameras and shoot miles and miles of film. What will you have obtained? A mountain of material in which are captured not only the essential aspects of an event but also the marginal and possibly absurd or ridiculous aspects. Your task will then be to reduce, to select. However, the real event also contained these aspects, it had the same marginal details, the same excess of material. By making a selection you are falsifying it. Or as some would say, you are interpreting it. It's an old argument. Life is not simple, nor is it always intelligible, and even the science of history is unable to express it in its entirety — a conclusion arrived at, via different paths, by both Strachey and Valéry, respectively a historian who made history into an art and a poet who despised history.

We have all heard of Pudovkin's experiments, in which he changed the meaning of a number of cinematic shots by changing the order of their appearance. A smiling man looking at a plate of soup is a glutton; if he looks at a dead woman with the same smile, then he is a cynic. But what, then, is the point of the eye at the keyhole, the two hundred cameras and the mountain of film? Today this type of cinema, which is based on Italian neo-realism, is known as *cinéma-vérité* or ' direct cinema '. Its defenders argue that it is completely objective, and from this we might suppose that its ideal tool would be the observing and describing camera devised by Silvio Ceccato, the director of the Cybernetics Centre at the University of Milan. But there is one fact which cannot be ignored, and that is that this camera, like any other, needs to be programmed. In fact it can operate from a number of different standpoints — a simply descrip-

11

tive one, another ethically evaluating one, another aesthetically evaluating, an explaining and commentating one, another sympathetic one, another antipathetic. And no doubt its uses will be increased in the future. In time, this camera could directly replace the commentator and reporter on newspapers. It may also be able to guide a motor car, but in this last case we should also have to inform it where we want it to get to. In other words, it needs a basis of orders and ideas.

The fact that *cinéma-vérité* directors walk around with a Coutant camera under their arm so that they can film their researches into other people's lives makes no difference at all. They still have to be guided by an idea, an attitude, without which their camera would remain inert, just as the most powerful computer in the world remains inert, in spite of its superhuman memory, so long as it is not supplied with a programme. Recently, in Paris, I went to watch the shooting of a film. They recorded a woman's replies to a number of questions put to her on the spur of the moment, then they transcribed these replies and made the woman learn them by heart, and after that they filmed the scene. One can imagine what an artificial result they must have ended up with.

In a village near Valdagno I stop for a drink in a bar. The building is situated on a very windy esplanade. The wind is particularly photogenic. There are other houses nearby, but they stand apart from one another, so that the wind blows between them, raising clouds of dust which swirl around me and then rise above the rooftops, appearing whiter still against the light. From inside the bar, the scene is even more evocative. A vast window enables one to see almost the entire esplanade, which is cut off in the background by a wall running horizontally across the landscape. The sky above the wall is blue, but seen through the dust it seems pale and washed-out. As the dust clouds drift away, it returns to its full intensity, like a mixture in solution. But a strange thing happens. I move around the room, looking for the right angle, but I can't find it. I would be very uncertain as to how I should frame what I see in a camera. Perhaps the difficulty arises from the fact that I haven't got a story to tell and so my visual imagination is working in a vacuum. I go

12

back to the bar, where a girl has in the meantime been getting me a drink. She's a fresh-looking girl with clear, melancholy eyes. She is probably about twenty-eight and is already beginning to lose her figure. Her movements are slow and precise. She is watching the scraps of paper and twigs being blown up by the wind outside. I ask her if it's always like this here. She replies: ' Absolutely.' Nothing more. She sits on a stool, leans her arm on the coffee machine and rests her head on her arm. She seems tired, sleepy or indifferent, or absorbed in serious thoughts. In any case she is motionless, and being thus motionless she starts to take on a character.

I think this is another way of making *cinéma-vérité* — to endow a person with a story, that is with the story which corresponds to their appearance, to their position, their weight, the volume they occupy in a particular space. Slowly, I move to the end of the bar counter, going round behind the girl so that she appears in the foreground. At the back of the room is the slanting window, with the dust clinging to the glass, then slowly dripping to the ground as if it were liquid. From here, with the girl in back view, a relationship between the external and the internal is established, the image takes on body. There is a meaning in the whiteness outside — an almost non-existent reality — and the dark patches inside, including the girl. She is an object too. A character without a face, without a story. The set-up is so beautiful that one hardly needs anything else to complete the impression.

Nevertheless I go up to her and while she is getting me another drink, I ask her what her name is. ' Delitta.' ' What? ' ' Delitta.' ' Like *delitto*? ' (A crime.) ' Yes, but with an a.' I look at her in amazement. ' It was my father,' she explains. ' He said it was a crime to bring a child into the world in his circumstances, but my mother wanted one so he said : " Very well, but we'll call it Delitto — a crime." And as I was a girl . . . That's how it was.' I could question her until I am exhausted, follow her step by step through the streets of her windy village and in her house which is no doubt clean and tidy — but I am sure that there would be no surprises in store for me, and that the one, the only, absurd extravagance in her life is her name — Delitta, like *delitto*, but with an a.

13

ANTONIONI — ENGLISH STYLE

' I want to re-create reality in an abstract form,' said Michelangelo Antonioni in an interview given during the shooting of *Blow-Up*. ' I'm really questioning the nature of reality. This is an essential point to remember about the visual aspects of the film, since one of its chief themes is " to see or not to see properly the true value of things ".'

Antonioni's attention to detail is well known. He is an absolute perfectionist as a director. He carefully controls everything in his work, down to the last detail. He uses the view-finder more often than most directors and sits in the operator's chair more often than the camera operator himself. Antonioni in fact almost always decides himself the framing and composition of the shots.

On the afternoon of the interview only one scene was being shot. There were twenty-one takes before Antonioni declared himself satisfied. The scene being shot was one in which Thomas (David Hemmings) and Patricia, played by Sarah Miles, come to verbal grips. It was a close-up of the actors in profile. They exchanged a few words, but Sarah Miles was responsible for dictating the rules of the game.

The worst enemy was noise. *Blow-Up* was shot in sync-sound and the non-existent sound-proofing in the photographer's studio did not help matters. The unfortunate din of traffic threatened to drown the actors' lines. The fourteenth take was terminated by a full peal of bells from a neighbouring church, which caused hysterical mirth on the set.

The twentieth take was perfect. Then the assistant director noticed that one of the crew members had slightly altered the set. The storm really broke then. Choking with anger, Antonioni cried out in desperation : ' The whole of London is against me ! '

The discussion scene between Thomas and Patricia amply defines the desperate and depressive mood of the film. Thomas and Patricia seem to live in a world of doubt — doubt which increases every day. They imagine that their lives are absolutely free, but they really are two magnificent cage-birds, prisoners in a whole system of ritual acts. They are looking for permanent values in an epoch which is characterized by permanent instability and the negation of all values. Patricia's replies in the conversation betray her fear and defeatism.

Antonioni looked tired. He admitted to sleeping badly during the shooting of his films. In addition, language difficulties made his task even more tiring. Antonioni does speak English quite well, but he preferred to give his more precise and detailed shooting directions in French for his interpreter to translate. The hazards of translation sometimes produced misunderstanding, which again wasted time.

A little later, in the studio, Sarah Miles had to give an embarrassed laugh after her last reply, but Antonioni wasn't satisfied with her effort. He turned to his interpreter who, it turned out, had confused the French word for embarrassed (*gêné*) with the word for generous (*généreux*). The translator also tried to make his point of view understood : ' But that smile was a typically British reaction.' Antonioni replied : ' I don't care ! I don't want a British smile . . . I hope nobody's going to say that *Blow-Up* is a typically English film. All the same, I hope nobody's going to say it's Italian, either.'

Originally the events of *Blow-Up* were to have taken place in Italy, but Antonioni finally decided that it was impossible to shoot it there.

' Firstly, a character like Thomas does not really exist in Italy. But the high-circulation newspapers in England really do employ photographers similar to the one I have portrayed in the film. Apart from which, Thomas is about to deal with a complex of events which could more easily happen in the life of London than of Rome or Milan. He has chosen to take part in the revolution which has affected English life, customs and morality, at least among the young — the young artists, trend-setters, advertising executives, dress-designers or musicians, who have been inspired by the Pop movement. He leads a life as regulated as a ceremony although he claims to know no other law but anarchy. I stayed some time in

15

London last year while Monica Vitti was filming *Modesty Blaise*. I realized then that London would be the perfect setting for a film like *Blow-Up*. But I don't want to make a film about London. The same events could happen in New York, maybe Stockholm, and certainly in Paris.'

For his exterior shots, Antonioni preferred a pale grey sky to a really pastel-blue one. He has tried to use a more realistic range of colours in *Blow-Up*, rather than attempting some of the artificial effects he tried in *The Red Desert*.

' I worked a lot then with the zoom lens to try and get two-dimensional effects, to diminish the distances between people and objects, make them seem flattened against each other. This time, I'm trying to do something quite different. I've tried to lengthen the perspective, to give the impression of space between people and things. I've only used the zoom lens when I've absolutely had to : for instance, when we had to shoot scenes in the middle of traffic jams. The greatest difficulty I have had has been the re-creation of the violence of reality. Colour always embellishes and softens what seems hard and aggressive to the naked eye.

' The more shocking elements in the film would also have made shooting in Italy impossible, because the censor would never have allowed some of the scenes. I've no doubt that censorship has become more tolerant in a lot of countries, but it remains just as rigid in the country of the Vatican.

' In *Blow-Up* there is, for instance, a scene in the photographer's studio in which two teenage girls behave particularly provocatively and end up completely naked. But I filmed this scene without any commercial intention at all and I don't think anyone could possibly describe it as obscene. The sequence is neither erotic nor vulgar. It's fresh, light and — I hope — funny. I can't stop people finding a shocking element in it, but I needed this scene in the film and I didn't want to give it up because it might displease some people.'

Perhaps at this point it is worth recalling something which Antonioni wrote in the preface to one of his scenarios : ' My films are not documents about a series of coherent ideas, but about ideas which spring up spontaneously.' For this reason he refused to com-

16

ment on his intentions in *Blow-Up*.

' I cannot possibly analyse one of my films until my work on it is completely finished. I am a film-maker with certain ideas which I hope to express with sufficient sincerity and clarity. I'm telling a story in this film. But whether it is a story which bears no relation to the world in which we live, I am incapable of deciding at this stage of the work.

' When I started to think about this film, I often stayed awake at night, thinking about it and taking notes. The story and its numerous possibilities eventually began to fascinate me, and I tried to think out where its various implications would lead me. But when I reached a certain point in my thoughts, I said to myself let's start shooting now and get the story down, then we'll see . . . And I'm still at that stage. To tell the truth, I'm not at all sure about what I'm doing. But I can have an inkling of it all the same because I'm in the secret.

' I think I work in a way which is both calculated and intuitive. A few moments ago, for example, I went off by myself to think about the next scene. I tried to put myself in the place of the protagonist when he finds the corpse. I walked over there on the grass, in the twilight, in the peculiar light of the neon sign. I got closer to the imaginary corpse and I felt a real identification with the hero of the film. I could just imagine the excitement and emotion which my hero would feel on the discovery of the corpse, how he was going to behave, react. This only lasted a minute or two. Then the rest of the crew came up and my inspiration and feelings just disappeared.'

Cahiers du Cinéma, January 1967

BLOW-UP – A MEMOIR

As the photographer in *Blow-Up* who never knows the identity of the murdered foreigner under the bush, so I never knew who Antonioni was when I met him. In a house in the Limehouse Docks, I was shooting with a 16-millemetre Bolex a scene for a short black-and-white film: it was to be used to cover set-changes in *Adventures in the Skin Trade*, my stage adaptation of Dylan Thomas's novel. A mutual friend of Antonioni's and mine, Claire Peploe, had brought him to visit the London docks, while he was scouting locations for *Blow-Up*. I did not hear her friend's name, which she mumbled as I prepared to start filming in my room on the Thames. "I'm busy," I said grandly. "I'm shooting. Wait".

With his usual grace, Antonioni waited. When I had finished my shot and discovered who he was, I was confused. I had told Antonioni to wait while I filmed my little piece of nonsense. It was worse than death by a thousand cutting-rooms. We had a brief conversation, translated by the enigmatic Claire. He praised the London scene and was intrigued by the Dylan Thomas play. He would come and see it, he said. He even quoted poetry in Italian that he claimed was written by Dylan Thomas, something about the pain and uncertainty of love being better than not being able to love at all.

We had asked Terence Stamp to play the Dylan role in our little play. He had refused. One of his reasons, I believe, was that he was being considered for the lead in *Blow-Up*. Instead, we chose David Hemmings, then little-known: he played the lead for the fortune of twenty pounds a week. His was a hallucinatory performance, compelling and imaginative. With his quality of beatific corruption, Hemmings looked too much the fallen angel for anyone's good.

I took Claire Peploe to the First Night of *Adventures in the Skin Trade*, and she took Antonioni to the Second Night. She wanted him to see the power of young Hemmings, who was immediately chosen by Antonioni to play the part of the photographer in *Blow-Up*. The loss of Hemmings prevented our play from transferring to the West End. His good fortune was our ill luck, although I myself was lucky. Tennessee Williams came to see the play and declared it was the best play running in London. Consequently, rather like Hemmings, I was offered a fortune to write a screenplay in Hollywood. So, as in the movies, sudden chance changed our lives.

David Hemmings was staying with me in my house on the river at Limehouse. He showed me the script of *Blow-Up*, what there was of it. It was a mere twenty pages, certain ideas of Antonioni and Tonio Guerra, hardly enough to hang a short film on. It would be invented in the shooting, David Hemmings said.

Soon a white Rolls Royce *coupé* was delivered, and Hemmings drove from the East End like King David. It was one of those fantastic changes of styles of living that characterised photographers like David Bailey in the late 1960's, the world of *Blow-Up*. Antonioni meant to capture the essence of 'swinging' London at the time, the sweet immorality of the women, the decadence without any visible future. As he said to Nadine Liber of *Life* magazine:– "Living among that youth, I had the precise sensation of entering a world which has finally put down barriers between individual and individual. No more taboo topics. I've talked to hundreds of girls and boys who were seeing me for the first time. If one is used to smoking marijuana, he'll say so without fear. If a girl is frigid, she'll have no inhibition to admit it. This is a generation that has approached a certain individual freedom . . . and freedom from feelings, too, because their sexual freedom, at this point, goes without saying. I don't know whether they can love the way we loved. They must suffer, I guess, but I'm sure they suffer from reasons very different from ours . . . never romantic. . . . To live as a 'swinger' . . . I think it means to take a lease from certain norms, certain traditions at any cost. . . . But maybe it is also a legitimate way to get nearer a happier condition of life. Who can tell?"

The shooting of the film depended on Antonioni's daily inspiration and improvisation. "When I was doing my first films," he said, "it would take me forty-five minutes of complete silence

19

and solitude to prepare for the next scene. Now I can isolate myself very easily. An actor must arrive on the stage in a state of virginity. I, too, must come to the set in a state of mental virginity. I force myself not to over-intellectualise. I force myself never to think the night before, of the scene I'll be shooting the next morning. I always spend a half hour alone to let the mood of the set, the light, prevail. Then the actors arrive. I look at them. How are they? How do they seem to feel? I ask for rehearsals – a couple, no more – and shooting starts."

A major role in *Blow-Up* was shot, featuring the foreigner first seen kissing Vanessa Redgrave, later found dead beneath a bush in the park. The role all ended on the cutting-room floor, leaving only the mystery of the blow-up sequence to prove that there had been a murder at all. In part, this treatment of the material reflected Antonioni's own ambivalence about the London people he was describing, where barriers were finally being put down between individual and individual. He was both attracted and repelled by English society with its quick engagement and speedy execution of those it engaged. He saw himself playing the part of the foreigner in his own film, then cut out his role and left himself rejected and probably betrayed by the elusive English *femme fatale* who led him to his fate. "Nothing like a little disaster," the photographer says to her, "for sorting things out."

Antonioni's *Blow-Up* has made history as well as cinematic history. Each time I see it, I am aware of that time, those places, such a style in bygone London. "I have never felt salvation in nature," Antonioni has said. "I love cities above all." He has inscribed London at that period for ever.

No director is more artistic and masterful than Antonioni. At one moment in the shooting of *Blow-Up*, his camera operator said that he could not follow a complex series of movements during a take. Antonioni himself sat at the camera controls with a pencil mounted on the lens and wrote his signature on a piece of paper by twiddling the right wheels. "If I can do that," he said to the operator, "you can shoot my shot." The operator heard, saw, and did so.

Above all, a master of the daily material he improvises or intuits from place and people and atmosphere, Antonioni captured in *Blow-Up* a period and urban manner that approaches *ciné verité*. Its successor, *Zabriskie Point*, remains too far out, too idiosyncratic to suggest more than an alien perception of the California of the time; but *Blow-Up* is so evocative that its images are more real to me than my own memories of those days. As oblique and insoluble as the murder of the foreigner was my own involvement in the making of *Blow-Up* – an encounter, consequences, marginal happenings. Yet so troubling and haunting is Antonioni's film that I am always seeing that time through his camera eye with David Hemmings's shutter open.

ANDREW SINCLAIR

CREDITS:

Screenplay by	Michelangelo Antonioni and Tonino Guerra; English dialogue in collaboration with Edward Bond Inspired by a short story by Julio Cortazar
Directed by	Michelangelo Antonioni
Produced by	Carlo Ponti
Executive producer	Pierre Rouve
Production company	Metro-Goldwyn-Mayer Inc.
Director of photography	Carlo di Palma
Music by	Herbert Hancock 'Stroll On' featured and conducted by the Yardbirds
Cameraman	Ray Parslow
Art director	Assheton Gorton
Dress designer	Jocelyn Rickards
Assistant director	Claude Watson
Production manager	Donald Toms
Location manager	Bruce Sharman
Sound recordist	Robin Gregory
Editor	Frank Clarke
Sound editor	Mike le Mare
Dubbing mixer	J. B. Smith
Continuity	Betty Harley
Dialogue assistant	Piers Haggard
Wardrobe supervisor	Jackie Breed
Hairdresser	Stephanie Kaye
Photographic murals by	John Cowan
Made on location in	London
and at	M.G.M. Studios, Boreham Wood
Colour by	Metrocolor
Length	9,974 feet
Running time	111 minutes
First shown in	New York, December 1966

22

CAST:

Thomas, the photographer	David Hemmings
The Girl (Jane)	Vanessa Redgrave
Patricia	Sarah Miles
Bill	John Castle
Ron	Peter Bowles
The Blonde	Jane Birkin
The Brunette	Gillian Hills
The Old Man	Harry Hutchinson
The Models	Verushka, Jill Kennington, Peggy Moffitt, Rosaleen Murray, Ann Norman, Melanie Hampshire
The Tennis Players	Julian Chagrin, Claude Chagrin

BLOW-UP

It is early morning in London. A group of shouting students dressed in bizarre clothes and with white powdered faces are loaded in a jeep which drives into a paved courtyard surrounded by modern buildings.[1]

Camera pans with the jeep as it comes towards us.

Camera pans with the shouting students in the jeep as it circles in the background.

Medium shot, panning with the jeep as it circles, then comes towards us again. The students are still shouting and waving as it drives off-screen.

Camera pans with the students in the jeep, which stops at the entrance to the square. The students go on shouting and laughing as they climb out of the jeep.

In St. James's Street, we see the shouting students as they run down some steps into the main thoroughfare. (Still on page 33) Camera follows them as they run along the street.

Camera follows the students as they run, shouting, down the middle of the street. A few of them stop and stare at something that we cannot see.

Outside the courtyard of Camberwell Reception Centre — a hostel for down-and-outs — a small crowd of ragged men is emerging from the main gate : old, young, all ages. Among them is a YOUNG MAN in his middle twenties, dishevelled and unshaven. He is carrying something in a tattered brown paper bag. (Still on page 33)

The group of men, including the YOUNG MAN, walk away towards a railway bridge as a train passes in the background along an embankment.

The men arrive at another set of gates giving onto the street, with the YOUNG MAN among them. He goes off to the right.

Back to the students, who are now stopping traffic in the street. The noise is deafening after the quiet of the previous scene. The students stop a white car, asking people for donations. They gather round a black car as well.

We see the group of down-and-outs under the railway bridge dispersing in different directions.
The YOUNG MAN in his middle twenties is standing under the archway near the hostel, with the parcel under his arm. Around him are three of the men who spent the night in the same place. The men move off after a few moments, muttering vague words of farewell to each other : ' *Well, see you, if you're back tonight . . .*' The YOUNG MAN looks carefully in every direction. Camera follows him as he turns the corner and walks away, hurriedly at first and then running, down the road towards a car parked some distance away.

Two nuns come through large gates and round the corner in front of St. James's Palace. Camera follows them as the students run forward, shouting, almost knocking them over. The nuns hurry past a guard in red coat and bearskin who is marching up and down outside the entrance to the palace.
A Rolls-Royce Silver Cloud convertible appears unexpectedly, driven by the YOUNG MAN from the Reception Centre. The students swing round the first corner and form a circle around it.
The YOUNG MAN laughs as three of the students shake their tin cans at him.

BOY : *Your money . . .*
    The YOUNG MAN rummages in the back seat amongst newspapers and the paper bag he had under his arm previously. The lens of an expensive camera can be seen sticking out of the brown paper bag.
The YOUNG MAN finds a pound note.
He gives the pound note to the three students.
GIRL : *Thank you!* The students run off.

The Rolls-Royce moves on in a different direction and slows at an intersection. Camera follows as it crosses the traffic going into a very dark underpass.

The YOUNG MAN is seen from above at the exit to the underpass, speaking into a radio-telephone placed under the dashboard. Camera tracks out in front of the moving car as he speaks:

YOUNG MAN: *Blue four-three-nine. Blue four-three-nine. Over.*

OPERATOR over: *Blue four-three-nine. Go ahead please. Over.*

YOUNG MAN: *Call Western oh-two-one-nine. Tell them I'm on my way, will you?*

OPERATOR over: *Roger. Wilco. Stand by.*

In a street in Kensington, we follow the Rolls-Royce as it pulls up in front of a black garage on which is painted a huge number 39. It is the YOUNG MAN's photographic studio.

The PHOTOGRAPHER's hands take a camera out of the brown paper bag. Camera tracks and pans to show him putting it in the glove compartment, locking it, then picking up the parcel and getting out. He goes towards the smaller, brown front door of number 39.

The PHOTOGRAPHER opens the door and disappears inside.

Inside the photographer's studio, the entrance hall has been fitted out as an office. The RECEPTIONIST, a beautiful Oriental girl, is working by a lamp, retouching a photograph. The PHOTOGRAPHER comes through the office as she sits down at a desk.

PHOTOGRAPHER: *Hello, love.*

RECEPTIONIST: *Hello.*

The PHOTOGRAPHER goes into the next room.

The upper floor can be reached either by crossing a vast room at street level or by climbing a narrow staircase leading straight into his private flat. The PHOTOGRAPHER takes the staircase, and camera follows him up.

He comes into a narrow passage-way, then into the kitchen. Here there is another young man, drinking coffee. He is one of the two assistants. The PHOTOGRAPHER takes several rolls of film out of the parcel and hands them to him.

PHOTOGRAPHER : *Get these developed, will you?*

ASSISTANT : *Yeah*.

In the background we glimpse two model girls dressing and putting on make-up. (Still on page 33)

Close shot of the PHOTOGRAPHER.

PHOTOGRAPHER to the ASSISTANT : *Right away*.

Then he opens the door to his living room-cum-studio and peers through.

Another model is reflected in a pane of plate glass propped up in the studio as he sneaks in and goes up to a table. He puts his cameras down and pours himself a glass of wine. (Still on page 34) The ASSISTANT passes through the studio with the films for developing. The sound of the MODEL'S voice makes the PHOTOGRAPHER turn around.

MODEL : *Here I am*.

PHOTOGRAPHER : *Ready?* He moves away.

The MODEL, wearing a black shawl, is sitting on a bench in the living area of the upstairs studio. She comes forward, stooping under a low beam.

MODEL : *I've been ready for nearly an hour!*

PHOTOGRAPHER off : *Good!*

The PHOTOGRAPHER is arranging the studio. The MODEL comes towards him.

MODEL : *I'm catching a plane for Paris at eleven, so I can't . . .*

PHOTOGRAPHER at the same time : *Can't what?*

The PHOTOGRAPHER is picking up some coloured ostrich feathers.

MODEL : *It doesn't matter*.

We follow the PHOTOGRAPHER as he moves closer to the MODEL. The PHOTOGRAPHER studies her : the MODEL looks a bit tired.

PHOTOGRAPHER : *Who the hell were you with last night?*

The MODEL smiles. She goes off.

PHOTOGRAPHER : *Reg!* He jerks his thumb up to the ceiling.

REG hurries across to open a blind covering the ceiling skylight.

28

Light streams in from the skylight, illuminating the MODEL as she takes off her shawl.

The PHOTOGRAPHER puts down the plumes and then takes off his shoes, looking towards her closely. Camera pans as he moves slowly towards her with the plumes — arranging them round her.

The MODEL is in front of a back-drop of paper. Her dark dress is loose and low-cut with slits down the sides. She is naked underneath. The PHOTOGRAPHER arranges the plumes on a rack beside her.

The MODEL stands in close shot with plumes fluttering round her.

The PHOTOGRAPHER stations himself behind the tripod with the camera on it, with REG beside him. (Still on page 34)

PHOTOGRAPHER : *Reg, let's have some noise.*

REG goes to put some music on and the PHOTOGRAPHER focuses his camera.

The music is jazz and rather sensual. The MODEL, standing in front of the back-drop with the plumes on the left, starts going into various poses, flexible and relaxed, giving the impression of a rubber-jointed doll. (Still on page 34)

PHOTOGRAPHER off : *Right.*

Resume on the PHOTOGRAPHER, who takes one or two shots.

PHOTOGRAPHER : *Yes, that's good, that's good, hold that.*

Resume on the MODEL with an arm outstretched — she sinks down slightly. The MODEL poses, and THOMAS photographs her, and throughout this sequence we hear the click of the camera shutter.

The MODEL from another angle — she pushes back her hair. Click.

The MODEL again — she lunges forward. Click.

Another shot of the MODEL, straightening up, then undulating her body in time to the music. Click.

Close-up of the PHOTOGRAPHER. The ASSISTANT sets up a new camera. The PHOTOGRAPHER, still watching the MODEL closely, takes a sip of wine.

Resume on the MODEL. The PHOTOGRAPHER then gets down on his knees, closer to her. More shots.

REG is loading another film into the first camera.

PHOTOGRAPHER off : *Reg!* REG looks up. He fetches another camera and hands it to the PHOTOGRAPHER, who slips the strap over his neck, his eyes still on the MODEL.

Close-up of the PHOTOGRAPHER seen from below, taking more shots.

Camera moves with him as he crouches down near her. They are both seen from above.

PHOTOGRAPHER : *Give us a smile. Come on. That's it. Yes.*

Then he goes closer to her, clutching the camera to his chest like a machine gun, taking one shot after another. (Still on page 35)

Closer and closer to her. They're both on their knees. A new record is on now, faster.

PHOTOGRAPHER : *Hunch. Hunch more . . . That's it . . . That's it . . . That's good.*

The MODEL is on the floor, and the PHOTOGRAPHER jumps around her, getting more and more excited. (Still on page 35)

He pushes her hair back.

PHOTOGRAPHER : *Now the hair back. Now the hair back.* He whispers in her ear. She smiles. *Come on, that's great. That's great! That's good. Good. Come on, more of that. More of that. Now, give it to me. Really give it to me. Come on, now!*

Camera follows him as he moves away and stoops in the foreground, taking more pictures.

Resume on the MODEL, seen in close-up over his shoulder.

PHOTOGRAPHER : *As quick . . . As . . .*

He moves away to get another angle.

PHOTOGRAPHER off : *. . . fast as you can. As fast as you can. Now give it to me. Give it to me! Come on. Right forward.* He reappears. *Good. That's good. Now, to get this side. This side. Lean right forward. Lean right forward.*

Now the PHOTOGRAPHER puts her hand up to her mouth. He begins taking pictures again.

30

PHOTOGRAPHER : *Hand up. Hand up. That's great. Just touch your face. That's very good. Now again, around this way. Around this way.* Camera pans as he moves to shoot her from another angle. *Half the face again — half the face again. Good. Now the hair. Now the hair.* He gestures and she loosens her hair. *Marvellous. That's great. Good. Yes, the hair . . . Much more. Much more. Good. That's great. Yes, that's great. That's good. That's good. Yes! Go on. That again. That again. That again.*

Resume on the MODEL in close-up, leaning her head back and shaking her hair. THOMAS takes pictures.

PHOTOGRAPHER : *Oh, hold that. Hold the hair — to the left. Again. Good.*

He gets to his feet, slips the camera off and hands it to his ASSISTANT.

PHOTOGRAPHER : *Okay, Reg. Fifty.*

REG passes him another camera. The PHOTOGRAPHER puts it over his shoulder and turns again towards the MODEL.

PHOTOGRAPHER : *You can relax. On your back. Go on. Yes. Now, really give it.*

The MODEL lies down on the floor. Camera moves in closer as she begins writhing her body slowly and knowingly. The PHOTOGRAPHER begins shooting her again.

PHOTOGRAPHER off : *Come on. Come on, work, work, work. Great. Great. And again. Come on. Back, back — arms up, arms up — stretch . . .*

He stands astride her and slowly bends his legs over her, still snapping one shot after another. Again he whispers in her ear and again the MODEL smiles, holding out her hands as if to caress him. The PHOTOGRAPHER is starting to get excited too. His movements are wild.

PHOTOGRAPHER : *. . . yourself, little lady. Great. And again. Go at it. Go, go. Great. That's it, keep it up. Lovely. Yeah, make it come. Great. Don't give up now. Yes, think of what I said to you. No, no. Head up, head up.*

We see the MODEL closer as she slowly sits up.

PHOTOGRAPHER : *Love, for me. Love, for me. Now, now . . .*

31

Thomas kneels over the Model. His voices rises to a crescendo.

PHOTOGRAPHER : *Yes, yes, yes . . .*

Then he stops, and the Model gives way to her exhaustion, lying back.

The Photographer gets up and slumps onto the divan. The Model stays stretched out on the floor in the foreground. (Still on page 35) The telephone rings. The Assistant goes and answers it, while the Model gets up and walks away, camera panning with her long, bare legs.

ASSISTANT off-screen : *Hello . . . Yeah, hold on.*

He comes back in and passes the telephone to the Photo- grapher.

ASSISTANT : *It's Peter.*

The Photographer takes the receiver.

PHOTOGRAPHER : *Hello? Hmmm? Yes. Yes. Yeah, I've got it some- where. I know I have. Huh? Yeah, hold on.*

He puts the receiver down on the table.

PHOTOGRAPHER : *Reg, take down the address of that bloody junk shop, would you?*

The Assistant comes over and takes the phone away.

The Photographer is shaving in the bathroom, seen through the doorway. He is now wearing a clean blue shirt and white jeans.

He rinses his face as the first Assistant comes in unexpectedly with the contacts of the photographs he has developed. The Photographer looks at them as he dries his face.

We see that the photographs are those taken in the Reception Centre : portraits of tramps, sordid surroundings, the scum of the earth surprised in their sleep.

PHOTOGRAPHER off : *Why, they're fabulous! Go on.* Camera tilts up to show Thomas and his Assistant looking at the pictures. *Yes. Yes. Great.*

He takes the tatty clothes he was wearing before off a stool and hands them to the Assistant.

PHOTOGRAPHER : *Here, you can burn that lot.*

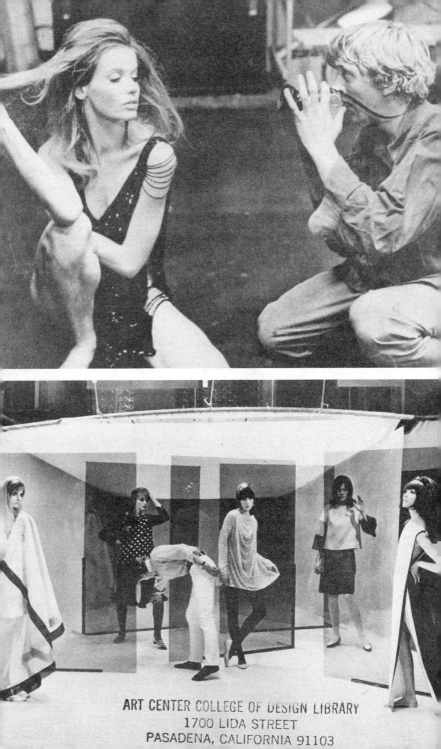

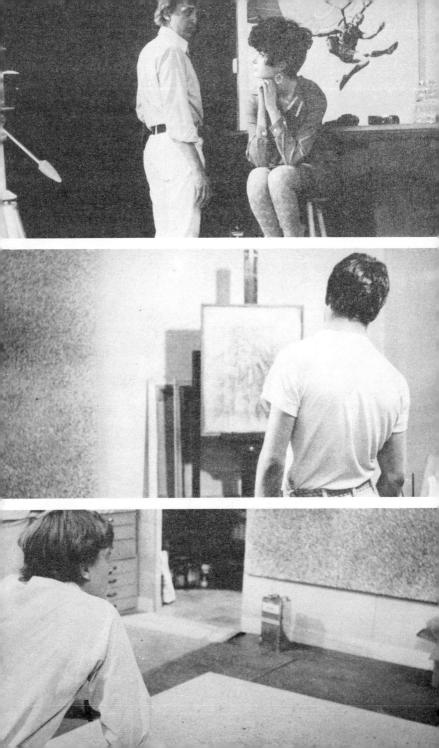

Camera pans as he leaves the bathroom, followed by the ASSISTANT, who looks surprised.

He retraces his steps of a few hours before when he came in. Strapping on his wristwatch, he enters a wide hall leading to the ground-floor studio. A jazz record is playing. The ASSISTANT throws the tatty clothes onto a box and then follows him. The PHOTOGRAPHER comes into the studio. Camera pans and tracks as he looks up towards a high window the length of the wall covered by a sheet of clear plastic, behind which a model can be seen dancing. He puts two fingers in his mouth, and whistles.

PHOTOGRAPHER shouting: *Reg!*

REG appears through a doorway at the top of the steps, just below the high window.

PHOTOGRAPHER off: *Get the birds down, will you.*

ASSISTANT: *Okay.* He disappears up the steps again.

All five models appear and look down, from behind the plastic sheet.

The PHOTOGRAPHER is standing down below in the studio where a white canvas back-drop with a false ceiling is hanging. Under the back-drop, panes of smoked glass as high as the ceiling have been arranged for the shots the PHOTOGRAPHER is going to take. The young man takes off his shoes and wanders thoughtfully amongst the panes of glass. (Still on page 36)

A dresser is giving the final touches to a model's dress, pinning the back with clothes pegs. The PHOTOGRAPHER comes in and stands behind his camera, positioned on its tripod, with his ASSISTANT. The woman dresser joins them.

Two of the models strike poses, seen from behind. One, wearing a long black and white tabard, chews gum; the other, in a silver dress and sequined cap, raises an arm.

PHOTOGRAPHER: *Oy! No chewing-gum. Get rid of it. And not on my floor.* She sticks the chewing-gum behind her ear. *You, arm down* . . . The other model lowers her arm. *All right.*

The ASSISTANT gives him a reading from the lightmeter. The PHOTOGRAPHER takes one picture. We see him between two of

41

the glass panels. Then he looks up.

PHOTOGRAPHER : *Terrible* . . .

The models stand posed against the back-drop. The PHOTO-GRAPHER comes up to one of them and grasps her leg.

PHOTOGRAPHER : *How about the leg a little further forward?*

He pulls the girl's leg forward, viciously, and says :

PHOTOGRAPHER : *Put the head up.*

She follows his instructions as he goes off behind a panel.

Camera pans across to the models, all posed differently.

The PHOTOGRAPHER goes back to his camera and takes some more shots. The model with blonde hair stands in the foreground, while another can be seen reflected in a glass panel. The models keep changing their poses. (Still on page 36)

PHOTOGRAPHER : *Just go . . . mouth open. Yes, good. Good.*

The model poses as instructed. We move on to another model beside her.

The model in the sequined cap looks dramatically towards the right. A fourth girl stands beside her swaying slightly to the music.

The model wearing the tabard scratches her head, assumes a surprised expression and leans back.

The PHOTOGRAPHER takes a few pictures.

Resume on the dramatically-inclined model crouching down, reaching out. Camera pans with her as she leans her head on her hand and stretches out a leg.

Resume on the PHOTOGRAPHER. He waves a hand.

PHOTOGRAPHER : *No, you're all lost. Start again. Start again. Re-think it.*

The models try again, adjusting their poses.

PHOTOGRAPHER off : *Re-think it.*

The PHOTOGRAPHER comes up to the blonde model, who stands holding out her dress, a long flimsy white cloak with black stripes over the shoulders. REG and the dresser look on indifferently.

PHOTOGRAPHER : *Stripes — let the dress just fall down.* She lets go of it. *Absolutely fall. Keep the stripes steady. It's very important to*

42

keep . . . Just let your arms go up . . . and down. He raises and lowers his arms to show her.

Now he is back behind the camera.

PHOTOGRAPHER: *Yes. Very tasty. Yes, I like it. I like it. Go on. Yup. All right, change positions.* He moves the tripod a few feet to the right. *Yup.*

He looks at the models. Their attention has strayed during the pause. He gives another strident whistle, with his fingers in his mouth, then yells:

PHOTOGRAPHER: *Wake up!*

The glass panes have now been moved into different positions, along an oblique line. The models have changed their outfits and are holding poses half-obscured by the panes of glass. Only their feet are plainly visible. Camera moves in towards them.

PHOTOGRAPHER off: *Now — you can thank your lucky stars you're working with me, can't you? All right, one more. Let's have a smile now. Come on. Smile! Smile!*

Camera moves across revealing all the models, then on farther to reveal the PHOTOGRAPHER taking pictures like mad. (Still on page 36) He goes up to the models, exasperated.

PHOTOGRAPHER: *God!*

He walks slowly past the models, addressing them all.

PHOTOGRAPHER: *I asked you to smile. What's the matter? Have you forgotten what a smile is?* Yelling at the last girl: *Eh?!* She flinches.

THOMAS starts to come back to his camera. He glances back at the girls: they are tired and show it.

PHOTOGRAPHER: *All right, you're all tired now. Go on, relax.*

The models relax and move away from the glass panels.

Pan across with two of them in close shot swaying to the music.

PHOTOGRAPHER off-screen: *I can't see your eyeballs any more. They're just slits. Go on, close your eyes.*

They close their eyes.

PHOTOGRAPHER off-screen: *Close your eyes. And stay like that. It's good for you.*

Camera pans across all five girls, closing their eyes.

GROUP, singing on record, over:

43

> *. . . Sometimes you really need a girl*
> *And you get distracted by her older sister*
> *Then in walks her father and takes you . . .*

THOMAS turns and goes to put on his shoes, camera following all his movements. He straightens up, gets his jacket and as he passes, tells the woman dresser to close her eyes.

PHOTOGRAPHER : *Close your eyes!* (Still on page 37)

He comes through the studio door into the hall that leads to the garage and picks up the pile of tatty clothes from the box. He then comes out into a yard at the back of the studio and tosses the clothes into the rubbish bin. He crosses the yard, swinging his jacket.

Quick shot of THOMAS, the photographer, as he goes towards another house on the far side of the yard.

The door of the other house is open. From inside we see THOMAS coming in. He closes the door behind him and tosses his jacket onto a chair. BILL's house is a modern, open plan building built round a patio, with nearly all the interior walls made of plate glass. THOMAS sinks into the chair in the hall-cum-living room, his hands clasped behind his neck.

From where he is sitting, he can see BILL at the door of his studio across the tiny patio. But instead of painting, BILL is absorbed in contemplation of a painting propped up on his easel. (Still on page 37) When BILL notices his friend is there, he nods towards him. The painting on the easel differs from those hanging on the walls and from an unfinished painting which lies on the floor. These are all abstracts made up of coloured dots. And yet they have a certain dramatic tension to them. The one on the easel is more figurative. That is to say, there is a figurative element in the painting. And it is on this that the painter has riveted his attention.

BILL is seen in close-up as he describes his painting, which can be seen over his shoulder in the studio.

BILL : *That must be five or six years old.*

As BILL moves forward, camera follows him to show THOMAS, who gets up and crosses the patio. He stands beside BILL, leaning on the doorpost. They both look at the painting.

BILL : *They don't mean anything when I do them — just a mess. Afterwards I find something to hang onto — like that — like — like . . .*

A closer view of the painting. BILL points at it.

BILL : *. . . that leg.*

BILL glances across at THOMAS.

BILL : *And then it sorts itself out. It adds up. It's like finding a clue in a detective story.*

He moves. His eyes fall on the picture lying on the floor. They both look at it.

BILL : *Ha . . . Don't ask me about this one. I don't know yet.*

THOMAS : *Can I buy it?*

BILL : *No.*

Another shot of BILL and THOMAS standing among the paintings. THOMAS leans his arm against the doorpost.

THOMAS : *Will you give it to me?* BILL shakes his head.

THOMAS squats down to study the painting on the floor. (Still on page 37)

He gets up and goes back to the chair he was sitting in before. PATRICIA, BILL'S young wife, comes down from the stairs that lead into the studio and sees THOMAS. Camera moves back as she goes over to the refrigerator in the kitchen. She is seen through the plate glass window that gives onto the patio.

She takes a bottle of beer out of the fridge, collects a glass, and camera tracks with her as she goes up to THOMAS and hands him the beer.

PATRICIA : *Here you are.*

THOMAS : *Hm. Thank you.*

PATRICIA moves behind him and starts ruffling his hair.

THOMAS : *Tight-faced bastard.* He raises his voice and looks in BILL'S direction, grinning. *He won't sell me one of his crappy paintings. Hm. I'll creep down one night and knock it off.* THOMAS leans back.

PATRICIA smiles. But then she looks serious and stops ruffling his hair.

45

Resume on THOMAS.

THOMAS : *Don't stop. It's lovely.*

Resume on PATRICIA.

PATRICIA : *You look tired . . .*

THOMAS off : *Mmmm.*

Resume on THOMAS, who drinks his beer. PATRICIA stands behind him.

THOMAS : *I've been all night in the doss house.*

He gets up. As he passes PATRICIA, he flips his hand through his hair — as if to ruffle it on purpose — then he leaves the house.

PATRICIA shuts the door after him, then turns and looks at her husband with a sigh.*

THOMAS walks into the hall at the back of the studio, hurrying past the studio door.

He opens the door of the receptionist's office and sees two teenage girls waiting there, one blonde and one brunette. They leap to their feet, smiling at him.

The RECEPTIONIST gets up, and camera follows her as she comes up to THOMAS.

RECEPTIONIST : *They say they've been asked to come here.*

THOMAS : *Not by me.*

One of the two girls comes up to him.

BLONDE : *Well, we weren't exactly asked . . .*

Medium shot of the PHOTOGRAPHER and the RECEPTIONIST, who stand looking at the two girls.

THOMAS annoyed : *Sorry, I'm busy.*

Then, turning to the RECEPTIONIST :

THOMAS : *They're printing some snaps for me upstairs; go and fetch 'em.*

The RECEPTIONIST goes to collect the prints. THOMAS sits down behind the desk. Camera moves in closer on the two girls.

BLONDE : *Couldn't you give us just a couple of minutes?*

THOMAS fiddles with some coins on the desk.

---

* End of reel 1.

THOMAS : *A couple of minutes? I haven't even got a couple of minutes to have my appendix out.*

Close-up of a coin as he rolls it over his fingers.

THOMAS sits with his feet up on the desk. He tosses the coin away and switches on the radio.

SINGER on radio :

> . . . *get you in a whole lot of trouble*
> *Didn't know you had troubles*
> *Got my feet in the water*
> *Caught you walkin' toward his daughter*
> *Get you in . . .*

The two teenagers stand and look at him. Then they move away as the RECEPTIONIST comes back with the prints.

SINGER on radio :

> . . . *whole lot of troble*
> *Wow*
> *Jubilee!*

The two girls still stand watching him as the RECEPTIONIST gives him the prints. THOMAS leafs through them, getting up as he does so. Camera pans to follow all his movements.

BLONDE : *Well, when can we come then?*

THOMAS : *Don't.*

He picks up his coat and is about to go out when he turns to the RECEPTIONIST and says :

THOMAS : *Are the others still waiting with their eyes shut?*

RECEPTIONIST : *Yes, they're waiting, but their eyes are open.*

THOMAS : *Good.*

He makes for the door, then turns round again.

THOMAS : *Tell them to shut them again.*

THOMAS comes out of the front door of number 39 and walks over to his Rolls-Royce. He throws the pictures onto the back seat, and jumps in behind the wheel. The two teenagers run out after him. The PHOTOGRAPHER slips his coat on and glances at the BRUNETTE's handbag, as they lean on the side of the car.

THOMAS : *You can get rid of that bag — it's diabolical.*

She hides the bag away at once. THOMAS starts the engine and drives away.

The two girls run after him for a bit, camera tracking back on the front of the car.

BLONDE : *Can't we come back this afternoon?*

But THOMAS is already speeding away. He turns on the radio. Jazz. The girls are left behind, standing on the kerb. THOMAS mouths the beat of the music.

Another street. Traffic. We move with THOMAS all the time. All the houses in this street are red.

Closer view of THOMAS driving. He drives in a somewhat fanciful style. Sudden spurts amidst the thickest traffic, when it is obvious that he will have to brake a few yards on. Sharp swings at the last moment before taking a curve, as if he had only then made up his mind to turn in that direction.

THOMAS drives through another street with a blue house.

The Rolls-Royce goes past buildings under construction. In the distance a huge, unlit, neon sign.

Camera moves past new buildings, then picks up THOMAS's car, following it down the street.

In a quiet little street, THOMAS turns round as he drives to look at a couple of queers walking a poodle.

The queers stop and look in the window of an antique shop. Camera moves back and round to reveal the Rolls-Royce rounding the corner and also coming to a stop in front of the shop.

THOMAS gets out of his car and crosses the street to the shop. The two queers go on their way.

THOMAS looks at them as they mince off, then he goes into the shop.

THOMAS comes inside the shop, closing the door. It is an unassuming little shop, cluttered with all sorts of things. THOMAS looks around, surveying and evaluating, rather than searching for a definite object.

THOMAS walks round the shop, camera following his gaze. An old man's face springs out from behind a wrought-iron partition. THOMAS watches it agog.

OLD MAN : *What do you want?*

THOMAS off : *Just looking around.*

OLD MAN : *There are no cheap bargains here. You're wasting your time.*

THOMAS and the OLD MAN confront one another.

THOMAS : *Well, I'll just have a look.*

The OLD MAN comes forward and side-steps THOMAS. He moves over to a bookshelf.

OLD MAN : *What are you looking for?*

THOMAS, after a brief hesitation : *Pictures.*

The OLD MAN takes a packet of dusty papers off the bookshelf. They are piled underneath some pictures.

OLD MAN : *No pictures.*

He blows the dust off the papers into THOMAS's face and returns behind the partition. THOMAS follows him, waving a hand to clear the air.

OLD MAN : *What kind of pictures?*

The OLD MAN puts the papers with some others. THOMAS appears beside him.

THOMAS : *Landscapes.*

OLD MAN : *Sorry. No landscapes.*

THOMAS looks at him and smiles. Right in front of them, standing on top of a bureau behind some small plaster busts, there is an old landscape painting. THOMAS brings the statues down out of the way.

A close shot of THOMAS removing a bust of Abraham Lincoln. The OLD MAN dusts his coat a trifle uncomfortably.

OLD MAN : *Sold. All sold.*

THOMAS leans back as the OLD MAN moves a couple of steps to one side. Camera follows THOMAS as he goes up to the OLD MAN.

THOMAS : *You're the owner?*

OLD MAN : *The owner is out.*

THOMAS : *Expecting him?*

The OLD MAN does not reply. He grunts as he blows the dust off a lamp. THOMAS makes his way over to the door.

Once outside, he stands for a few moments on the kerb surveying the façade of the house over the shop. Then camera pans as he crosses the road towards his car. As he does so we see the gates to a path of velvet green grass and tall trees swaying in the wind.

A closer view as he takes the camera out of the glove compartment.

He walks out into the middle of the road and takes some shots of the shop from different angles. (Still on page 38)

Then from between the tall tree-trunks in the park we see him in the distance outside the gates. He turns and gazes at the trees. He moves towards the gates. A single bird sings, its song echoing loudly in the quiet park.

A council worker is picking up litter from the grass. THOMAS passes him, stops and looks about, then moves on. The man continues his work.

The park is bathed in a beautiful, soft light. Apart from the black rectangles of two tennis courts surrounded by high wire netting and two beds of white roses, there is nothing but greenness all around. In the midst of this greenness a white patch stands out in the background : a row of houses set amongst the trees. As THOMAS passes, carrying his camera, two boys are playing tennis on one of the courts. The sound of the racquets and the murmur of the birds and the wind only accentuate the sense of peace in the park.

Close-up of THOMAS squinting through the viewfinder, adjusting the lens.

THOMAS comes out into a wide clearing below the white houses. He starts taking some shots of a flock of pigeons on the grass. (Still on page 38) He runs about, snapping pictures of the fluttering birds.

THOMAS takes pictures of one pigeon as it flies off over the trees. Camera pans with it, allowing a glimpse of a MAN and a GIRL near the trees.

THOMAS comes forward and stops in the middle of the clearing, looking up.

The MAN and the GIRL are climbing up the wooded slope. They are holding hands and laughing, then they slip and fall, teasing and flirting with each other. The GIRL is doing her best to persuade the MAN to follow her up the slope to the top of the hill. The MAN seems somewhat reluctant to do so.

There are paths cut through the trees, with low wide steps leading up to the hill. THOMAS walks along a path, then runs up, leaping and kicking his feet like a Cossack dancer. Leaping from one step to another, he reaches the top of the slope.

Camera tilts down the shallow steps as THOMAS comes up. The slight friction between the two strangers has aroused THOMAS's curiosity. He follows them as discreetly as possible. He peers between branches, focusing his camera.

A tiny meadow enclosed by trees. Utterly peaceful. Only the rustling of the leaves in the wind. And over to one side the same couple, totally unaware of THOMAS's presence.

The couple is far away, one in front of the other. The GIRL is pulling the MAN by the arm. She is laughing at the same time. From where THOMAS stands she looks attractive and graceful. THOMAS leaps over the wooden fence running round the meadow and aims his camera.

From behind the fence he takes pictures from all angles. But he is too far away from the couple.

He moves closer, edging along behind the fence, ducking under a branch, then taking some more photographs.

A brief glimpse of the couple.

THOMAS climbs over the wooden fence again and hides behind a tree in the foreground. A few more photographs from this position. But he is still too far off.

THOMAS snaps the couple in the distance as they kiss but he doesn't have his telephoto lens with him.

Cautiously he moves behind another tree closer to the couple. (Still on page 38)

The GIRL has brought the MAN out into the middle of the meadow. She kisses him, then they drop hands and she moves off. She seems to let her eyes wander over the landscape, drinking in its peacefulness.

THOMAS has taken enough photographs, and moves closer. We see him way back at the edge of the clearing, sidling towards another tree.

Meanwhile the GIRL has moved on. She has succeeded in drawing the MAN farther up, towards the other side of the small clearing. And again she embraces him and kisses him.

THOMAS moves away from his hiding-place at the far end of the clearing. Hardly realizing what he is doing, he stops again and snaps them. Then he makes his way back to the same path he came up on.

The GIRL and MAN have suddenly noticed him. They are watching him rather anxiously. THOMAS starts to disappear down the slope. The GIRL begins running after him, reaches the path, and stops.

THOMAS pauses when he hears her running, and turns round. He sees the GIRL, instinctively holds up his camera and takes some more shots. (Still on page 39)

GIRL off : *What are you doing?*

The GIRL stands at the top of the steps, holding her hand out defensively. She rushes down towards THOMAS with barely concealed anger, going a few steps below him.

GIRL : *Stop it! Stop it! Give me those pictures. You can't photograph people like that.*

THOMAS lowers his camera, and looks round at her with a friendly smile.

THOMAS : *Who said I can't? I'm only doing my job. Some people are . . . bull-fighters. Some people are politicians. I'm a photographer.*

They stand looking at one another.

GIRL : *This is a public place. Everyone has the right to be left in peace.*

THOMAS goes and leans against the fence, camera moving after him. (Still on page 39)

He studies her curiously. She stands there rigid, her lips tight.

THOMAS : *It's not my fault if there's no peace. You know, most girls would pay me to photograph them.*

THOMAS stands looking down at the GIRL.

GIRL : *I'll pay you.*

THOMAS : *I overcharge. There are other things I want on the reel.*
He turns and looks up towards the meadow, then hurries up
the steps. Camera moves across to the GIRL.
THOMAS comes up to the edge of the clearing and looks at the
spot where the MAN was standing a moment ago.
The GIRL follows him up the steps in confusion.

GIRL with a touch of hopelessness : *What do we do, then?*
Another shot of them both. She is very agitated.

THOMAS : *I'll send you the photographs.*

GIRL : *No, I want them now.*
She suddenly snatches at the camera and tries to wrench it
from THOMAS's hands. But he is quicker. He holds the strap
and doesn't let go. So the GIRL gets down on her knees.
She gives him a vicious bite on the hand.
THOMAS pulls away angrily. He shouts :

THOMAS : *No! What's the rush?*
Close-up of the GIRL looking up. (Still on page 39)
Resume on THOMAS recovering his poise. He goes on in a
different, rather ironical tone of voice :

THOMAS : *Don't let's spoil everything. We've only just met . . .*
He stands looking down at her. She gets up wearily. She is
desperate.
She steps back from him.
She raises her eyes and looks the YOUNG MAN straight in the
face, still moving away, and panting with anxiety.

GIRL : *No, we haven't met. You've never seen me.*
THOMAS bends down and picks up the lens cap of his camera.
As he screws it on he looks at something in the clearing. The
GIRL turns and looks in the same direction : the MAN has dis-
appeared. She seems annoyed.
She starts running away across the meadow to join the MAN
wherever he might be, and stops near a clump of bushes, paus-
ing a moment, then running on.

53

THOMAS takes a few more photographs of her.
The GIRL runs away and disappears down the other side of the hill.[2]

Through the doorway of the antique shop we can see THOMAS crossing the road towards it. A girl pushes a pram towards the park gates. Outside the shop window THOMAS meets the OLD MAN, who waves him in. He moves towards the door. An ancient recording of Hawaiian music can be heard.
In the back of the shop the owner, a girl, is sitting on a table, listening to an old record of Hawaiian music. She is very young, and dark-haired. THOMAS goes up to her. She hardly gives him a glance.

THOMAS : *Hello.*

GIRL : *Hello.*

She doesn't turn round, but changes the record. (Still on page 40)

THOMAS : *Uh — my agent saw you about the shop.*

GIRL rather vague : *Did he?*

THOMAS : *He's a man with a cigar. Throws ash everywhere.*

GIRL : *I expect I remember him. I probably asked for too much money. Money's always a problem, isn't it? Tell him to come back.*

She starts the gramophone again.

THOMAS goes up to her and, clasping her by the shoulders, swings her round to face him.

THOMAS : *Why are you selling?*

The GIRL switches off the gramophone.

THOMAS watches as she gets up and moves past him. Camera pans to follow her.

GIRL : *I'd like to try something different. Get off somewhere. Oh, I'm fed up with antiques.*

THOMAS off : *Get off where?*

GIRL : *To Nepal.*

THOMAS looks round the shop.

THOMAS : *Nepal is all antiques.*

GIRL off : *Is it?*

54

He nods his head.

THOMAS : *Uh-huh.*

Resume on the GIRL.

GIRL : *Perhaps I'd better try — Morocco.*

Resume on THOMAS, who grins. He strolls around looking at the various objects in the shop, piled one on top of the other. Some of them are rather fine. Something suddenly attracts his attention in the back room of the shop.

THOMAS : *How much?*

GIRL : *What?*

THOMAS : *The propeller.* He goes through to the other room, followed by the GIRL.

She comes into the room and leans against the wall.

GIRL : *You can have it for — eight pounds.*

THOMAS walks across to a huge, vintage aeroplane propeller made of wood, hidden under a pile of bits and pieces. He begins to clear the débris away from it.

THOMAS : *Right. You're in business. Have you got a van?*

GIRL off : *You can't take it now.*

THOMAS starts clearing a space around the propeller to shift it.

THOMAS : *I must. I must. I can't live without it.*

The GIRL comes and helps him clear the junk, laughing.

GIRL : *Hard luck. That'll teach you to fall in love with heavy things on Saturday morning.*

THOMAS lifts up an armchair to see the propeller; the chair fills the frame, blotting everything else from view.

THOMAS comes out of the shop door, carrying one end of the huge propeller. He goes off as the GIRL comes out carrying the other end.

Camera follows her as they cross the street.

GIRL : *Is that it?*

THOMAS : *That's it.*

They go up to the Rolls-Royce. THOMAS loads the propeller in the back seat, trying to arrange it so that it won't fall.

GIRL : *You can't treat it like that! It's not a delivery van.*

THOMAS : *Who cares?*

55

GIRL : *Leave it to me.* She shrugs. *Something will turn up.*

THOMAS : *Yes. All right. But it'd better turn up today. Bye-bye.*

He gives her back the propeller. It is far too heavy for her to carry alone and she cannot help dropping it on the ground with a clatter. THOMAS swings round.

THOMAS : *Oy!*

Then he gets in the car and starts the engine.*

The Rolls-Royce shoots out of a side street into heavy traffic, following a bus.

Buses in the street. Camera moves in to THOMAS driving among them.

THOMAS drives out of sight.

Up ahead we glimpse THOMAS driving through Hyde Park, camera moving in towards the car. This is how the car would appear to a vigilant but hidden eye, determined never to let it out of sight, keeping hot on its trail.

The car dives between a collection of skyscrapers.

THOMAS passes a bus. Track in as the bus stops and THOMAS drives on.

THOMAS relaxes as he drives, camera tracking ahead of him. He picks up the microphone and speaks into it.

THOMAS : *Blue four-three-nine. Blue four-three-nine. Over.*

OPERATOR off : *Blue one-two-six. Go ahead please. Over.*

THOMAS : *Hello, this is . . . uh . . . Get me Flaxman six-one-seven-seven. Mister Walker, Peter Walker. Tell him I've seen the junk shop. It's a bit pricey but the kid'll come down. Tell him to ring her straight away, then nobody else'll get it.*

OPERATOR off : *Roger. Wilco. Stand by.*

THOMAS puts the receiver back. The car turns into another street. The voice comes over the radio-telephone again. Camera moves in closer.

OPERATOR off : *Blue four-three-nine. Blue four-three-nine. Over.*

THOMAS picks up the receiver again.

THOMAS into receiver : *Blue four-three-nine. Blue four-three-nine.*

---

* End of reel 2.

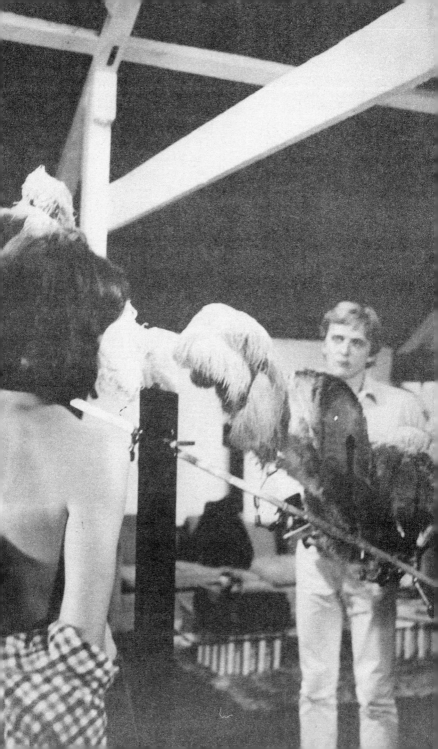

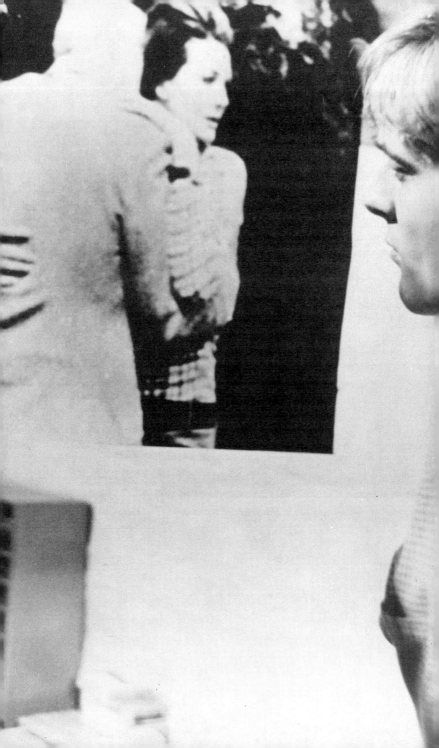

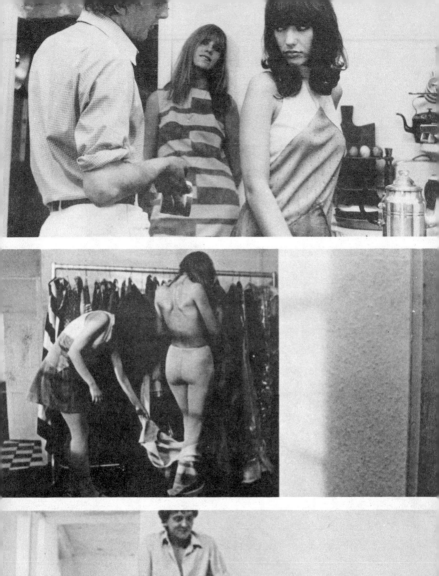
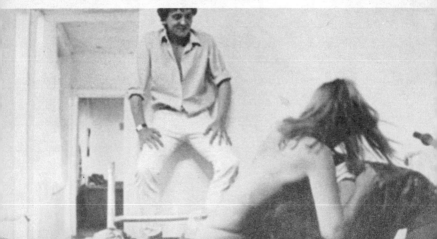

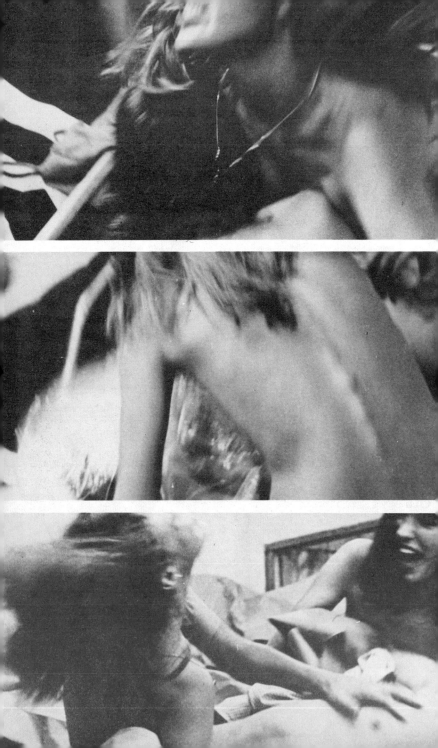

Go ahead, echo.
OPERATOR off : *Blue four-three-nine. Message passed to him at the studio. Your caller doesn't like it. Over.*
THOMAS : *Tell him to get stuffed . . . What about the buildings going up around the place? Already there are queers and poodles in the area. I saw some in the couple of minutes I was there. It'll go like a bomb. Over.*
OPERATOR off : *Blue four-three-nine. What is in the area? Over.*
THOMAS : *Forget it. Over.*
OPERATOR off : *Roger. Wilco. Standing by.*

THOMAS puts down the receiver.

The Rolls-Royce swings round a corner into the street outside a restaurant and pulls up at the kerb.

THOMAS gets out of the car. He picks up the prints from the back seat, and crosses the street to the restaurant.

The restaurant is full of people eating, drinking and chatting animatedly. THOMAS comes in, and goes straight to a table by the window where RON is waiting for him. He sits down. RON is a writer in his mid-thirties; he has a beard. THOMAS gives him the pictures. RON starts leafing through them.

RON : *You want to use the lot?*

THOMAS takes a gulp from RON's drink while RON goes on looking at the photographs.

Close-up of the photographs held over the table by RON's hand : one of men in the Reception Centre dressing; a man waiting behind a cracked window; a man sitting beside a bed in a dormitory; a naked man picking up some clothes. This picture is straightened by RON's hands. We hear RON and THOMAS discussing them, over.

THOMAS off : *Don't you like them?*
RON off : *They're great.*

Resume on RON and THOMAS at the table.

THOMAS : *We'll use three or four.*
RON : *Spread through the book?*

THOMAS sits back, revealing RON looking at one of the photographs.

THOMAS : *No, all together.*

RON : *Yes.*

> A WAITER is carrying some plates across to another table. Camera pans past RON as THOMAS stops the WAITER, and looks at what is on one of the plates. He points it out to the WAITER, gesturing that he would like some himself. THOMAS sits down with RON again.

THOMAS to the WAITER : *And a pint.*

WAITER : *Yes sir.*

> RON has picked up the dummy of the book of photographs he has with him.

RON : *Which one last?*

> Close-up of THOMAS. He leans forward.

THOMAS : *None of this lot. I've got something fab for the end. In the park. I only took them this morning. You'll get them later on today. It's very — peaceful. Very still . . . Well, the rest of the book'll be pretty violent so . . .*

> RON goes on leafing through the dummy full of photographs. Poverty-stricken creatures, layabouts, alcoholics, the bizarre and the absurd. We see the photographs in close-up as the writer and the photographer discuss the book off-screen.

THOMAS off : *I think it's best to end it like that. Hm?*

RON off : *Yeah. That's best. It rings truer.*

> Close-up of THOMAS glancing out of the window, parting the slats of the venetian blind with his hand. Camera moves back slightly.
>
> Camera moves in again on the two of them, THOMAS still staring out of the window.

THOMAS : *I'm going off London this week.*

RON : *Why?*

> He gazes outside as well.

THOMAS : *It doesn't do anything for me.* RON sees what THOMAS is looking at — a girl on the other side of the street.

RON laughing : *Ye-es!*

> They return to the photographs.

RON : *I've knocked up a few captions.*

THOMAS : *Yeah?*

He is distracted by a beautiful blonde coming through the restaurant. She is wearing slacks and moves like a model. Camera follows her, watched by the two men. THOMAS turns back to RON.

THOMAS jerking his head in her direction : *I'm fed up with those bloody bitches.*

Resume on THOMAS and RON.

THOMAS : *I wish I had tons of money. Then I'd be free.*

RON : *Free to do what? Free like him?*

Close-up of a photograph of an old man on a plot of derelict land — dirty, witless, a human wreck.

Resume on RON and THOMAS. Their attention is drawn to someone outside the window.

RON : *Someone we know?*

Through the venetian blinds beside their table, RON and THOMAS watch a MAN turn and walk hurriedly away across the street. He is a tall, fair-haired young man, dressed in black. He seems annoyed at being caught spying on them.

A wider view of the restaurant, with RON and THOMAS looking out of the window. THOMAS jumps up, and camera follows him as he hurries across to the door, opening it.

THOMAS comes out of the restaurant. He is surprised to see the stranger fumbling with his car, as if trying to force open the boot.

The stranger sees THOMAS and quickly makes off, mingling with a group of Africans, in national dress, on the pavement. Camera follows him as he passes them and gets into another car parked in a side street.[3]

Close-up of THOMAS watching the stranger's movements.

THOMAS crosses the street to his Rolls-Royce.

Camera pans as he checks that the boot is still locked, then he gets in the car and drives off, hooting at the Africans who have strayed off the pavement into the road.

A group of demonstrators with a policeman walking in front of them are crossing the road. They are carrying placards with slogans: GO AWAY; PEACE NOT WAR; NOT OUR LADS; NO! NO! NO!

The demonstrators cross the street, and camera follows as the policeman steps up onto the kerb.

The demonstrators start to wander across the road. THOMAS drives up and stops for them, holding up the traffic as he waves them across in front of the Rolls-Royce. Cars held up behind begin to hoot impatiently.

A girl comes up to the Rolls-Royce and slips a placard into the back, tucking it into the folded hood cover, just as THOMAS begins to move again. On it are the words: GO AWAY. Traffic passes him, hooting.

THOMAS turns and secures the sign, then smiles at the girl.

THOMAS : *That'll be all right.*

He drives off, followed a few seconds later by a gun-metal Rover 2000.

Seen in a closer shot, the placard flies off the back, but the photographer does not even notice. Camera tracks back and we see another car drive over the placard, splintering it.

It is early afternoon. The Rolls-Royce drives into the street outside THOMAS's studio, but cars are parked tight along the kerb. He has to drive the Rolls-Royce right down to the end to find a parking space. THOMAS gets out, with his camera, and slams the door. There is no one about. It is Saturday afternoon and the small street is buried in an almost funeral silence, save for the blaring of a television set: a man's voice discussing racing form.

For a moment THOMAS stands looking around in the quiet street. Then he goes and presses hard on the car horn.

THOMAS stands with his hand on the horn. The strident blast reverberates all along the street but nothing happens. THOMAS releases the horn and walks away.

One man appears at his garden gate: he is more amazed than anything else. THOMAS waves to him and skips off, camera panning with him.

THOMAS walks the distance between the car and his studio,

looking about.

He goes towards the front door of 39, then changes his mind and starts to cross the road.

There is a telephone booth opposite his studio, on the pavement. THOMAS goes in and dials the operator, camera moving in closer as he does so. When the operator answers, he says :

THOMAS : *Hello. Could you get me Frobisher three-double-two-nine, please? I've only got a sixpence . . . Park one-two-nine-six.*

He waits a moment. When he gets an answer at the other end he goes on :

THOMAS : *Hello, it's me . . . Weren't you supposed to be going off to — um — Purley? Mm? Listen . . . Stay where you are. Call me soon at home . . . Hm.* He hangs up.

THOMAS comes out of the phone booth. A few more steps — and he is home. He pulls out his key and is about to unlock the door. The clatter of a woman's hurried footsteps drawing near makes him turn round. A GIRL runs towards him.

It is the GIRL from the park. She is out of breath, and for a moment can hardly speak. THOMAS looks at her in surprise. Finally she says :

GIRL : *I . . . I've come . . . I've come for the photographs.*

THOMAS eyes her curiously.

THOMAS : *Well, how did you manage to find me?*

The GIRL avoids his eyes.

GIRL : *Do you live here?*

THOMAS : *Mmm.*

THOMAS opens the door and lets her in.

Through a partially open door in the foreground we see first the GIRL, then THOMAS coming into the studio through the front door. She comes through the second door, followed by THOMAS. Camera follows them as they go through the receptionist's office.

They come through the door into the large studio.

At the other end of the studio THOMAS closes the door. The GIRL comes forward, looking about with interest. She seems on edge. THOMAS joins her and we follow them as they walk

69

behind the smoked glass panels and up the steps at the back of the studio. (Still on page 57)

The GIRL and THOMAS come up the stairs to the upper studio. Camera moves with her as she comes forward, stooping under photographic equipment and ostrich plumes. THOMAS switches on a few scattered lights, motions to her to sit down, and switches on the record player. The music is a very slow guitar.

THOMAS : *Drink?*

She wanders about as if looking for something.

Without waiting for her answer he pours two whiskeys, and turns in her direction with the glasses.

THOMAS : *What's so important about my bloody pictures?*

Camera follows THOMAS as he goes up to her, now settled on the couch, to give her the glass. She holds him with her eyes. (Still on page 57) Doesn't take the glass.

GIRL : *That's my business.*

THOMAS puts her glass down. She gets up and stands stiffly opposite him. Both are obscured by an overhead beam.

Close-up of THOMAS, drinking and saying as if recollecting a pleasant memory :

THOMAS : *The light was very beautiful in the park this morning. Those shots should be very good. Anyway, I need them.*

Close-up of the GIRL leaning against a cross-beam. She is tense, insisting . . .

GIRL : *My private life's already in a mess. It would be a disaster if* . . . She moves away.

THOMAS comes across to the beam where she is standing and stares at her.

THOMAS : *So what — nothing like a little disaster for sorting things out.*

The GIRL starts at his reply. She paces up and down in front of the long polythene-covered window, growing more and more restless. Camera moves back to reveal THOMAS watching her with a professional eye through the beams of the low ceiling, then moves in again to the GIRL.

70

THOMAS off : *Have you ever done any modelling? Fashion stuff, I mean?*

The GIRL shrugs and sighs impatiently.

THOMAS off : *You've got it.*

Camera moves back to reveal THOMAS as she begins to wander about again. He studies her from head to toe, then moves across to the plastic-covered window. He motions her to come closer, pulling down a lilac-coloured back-drop in front of it. He stands her against the back-drop.

THOMAS : *Hold that.* He hurries away, leaving her standing rather bewildered.

THOMAS watches the GIRL standing impatiently in front of the screen.

THOMAS : *Not many girls stand as well as that . . .*

She comes towards him.

GIRL : *No thanks, I'm in a hurry.*

THOMAS takes off his coat, and heads for the couch.

THOMAS : *You'll get your pictures. I promise. I always keep my word.*

He falls onto the couch.

THOMAS : *Come here. Show me how you sit.*

Close-up of the GIRL. She sighs, but complies.

She goes and sits beside him.

THOMAS doesn't take his eyes off her. They sit side by side and he is relaxed and confident, just staring at her, satisfied that he has at least made her sit down. The telephone rings. He looks round at the sound but does not make a move. It goes on ringing.

THOMAS sits on the sofa, ignoring the telephone. He is seen from above, over one of the beams. Suddenly he hurls himself across the floor and dives for the telephone. He has to crawl behind an armchair to find it and bumps his head on a corner of the chair's wooden frame in the process.

THOMAS into phone, rubbing his head : *Who is it?*

Close shot of THOMAS.

THOMAS remembering his earlier call : *Oh yes, that's right. Hold on*

71

a second.

He stretches up and holds out the receiver. (Still on page 57)
Thomas's hand holds the receiver out from behind the chair.
He is otherwise invisible. Seen reflected in a large pane of glass,
the GIRL sits forward, shocked.

GIRL : *Is it for me?*

She goes over to him and sits in the armchair, camera moving
with her. Hesitantly she picks up the receiver.

THOMAS : *It's my wife.*

Close-up of the GIRL, hurriedly putting the receiver down, and
starting to rise.

GIRL : *Why should I speak to her?*

Close-up of THOMAS. He takes the receiver back and addresses
the person at the other end of the line, as the GIRL walks away
in front of him.

THOMAS : *Sorry, love, the bird I'm with won't talk to you.* He
hangs up.

The GIRL stands with her back to him, looking out of the
window. THOMAS moves over to her, but she moves away,
ducking under a beam. Camera moves in to close-up as she
turns and taps her knuckles impatiently on the beam.

THOMAS goes up to a painting in the living area, runs his finger
over it, then turns back to the GIRL, explaining :

THOMAS : *She isn't my wife really. We just have some kids . . .
No . . . No kids. Not even kids. Sometimes, though, it . . . it
feels as if we had kids. She isn't beautiful, she's . . . easy to live
with.*

He sits down in close-up and lights a cigarette.

THOMAS : *No she isn't. That's why I don't live with her.*

He breaks off, and drops a match on the lace mob-cap of a
marble bust on his right. It's a girl's head, and he gazes at
it, patting it thoughtfully as though reflecting on his personal
problems.

The GIRL stands behind some lighting equipment. She shows
a first minimal sign of interest in him. A moment of silence.
The GIRL goes and sits down on the couch again.

72

The YOUNG MAN gets up and goes on speaking, turning in her direction.

THOMAS : *But even with beautiful girls you . . . you look at them and . . . that's that. That's why they always end up by . . .* He sighs *. . . Well, I'm stuck with them all day long.*

THOMAS stands looking down at the GIRL on the sofa.

GIRL : *It would be the same with men.*

He shrugs. A new track is playing. This one has a fast beat.

THOMAS : *Have a listen to this!*

He moves up to the record player, and turns up the volume.

Close-up of THOMAS as he straightens. Pan and track with him as he moves with the music.

The GIRL listens. Instinctively she starts swaying with the rhythm. THOMAS goes and sits down beside her.

THOMAS motions her to listen to the music.

THOMAS : *No, keep still. Keep still! Listen. Keep still.*

A pause. He hands her the cigarette he is smoking.

THOMAS : *You can smoke, if you like.*

The GIRL takes the cigarette and in the same movement raises it to her mouth, still swaying in time to the music.

THOMAS : *Slowly, slowly. Against the beat.*

The GIRL tries to smoke moving slowly, swaying sensuously.

THOMAS off : *That's it.*

For a few minutes the GIRL stays with the game. She even seems a little amused. She returns the cigarette to THOMAS's hand, laughing.

THOMAS, in turn, draws on the cigarette very slowly, his eyes fixed on her, then gives to back to her.

Resume on the GIRL. She is about to take it, but changes her mind.

The GIRL gets to her feet abruptly : her nerves cannot stand such an artificial game. THOMAS gets up, too.

GIRL : *Ohhh . . . I can't stand it. I'm nervous enough as it is.*

She sits down again. Rummages in her bag. Then in a different voice she says :

GIRL : *Can I have some water?*

THOMAS : *Sure.* He goes off to the kitchen.

She watches him disappear into the kitchen, and immediately her eyes light on the camera lying on the film storage cabinet in the extreme foreground.

An instant's pause. She looks furtively towards the kitchen door, and then she is on her feet. She picks up her bag, then tiptoes over to the camera and picks it up.

She hurries past the ostrich feathers on tiptoe and rushes down the stairs leading through the great ground floor room towards the entrance hall.

The door downstairs is flung open and the GIRL bursts through. She stops dead in her tracks.

In front of her is the PHOTOGRAPHER. He is leaning against the wall, smiling slyly. He comes up to her at once, holding out his hand.

THOMAS : *And I am not a fool, love.*

The GIRL hands him back the camera. She leans against a counter top at the end of the big studio. Beside her is a huge blow-up of a girl doing a parachute jump.

GIRL : *Can I have the photographs?*

They stand looking at one another silently for a few moments.

THOMAS : *Of course. Later.*

They move towards the stairs again. She in front, he following.

THOMAS : *Your boyfriend's a bit past it.*

The GIRL goes on up the stairs without reacting, camera moving up with her.

No sooner are they in the studio than she turns and looks THOMAS straight in the face. It is obvious she resents his previous remark.

GIRL : *Why don't you say what you want?*

They stand looking at one another, the rack of ostrich feathers between them. THOMAS avoids having to answer. The GIRL puts down her bag and starts undoing her blouse.

The GIRL stands behind the ostrich plumes and takes off her blouse. (Still on page 58) She is not wearing a bra and stands there bare-topped, but with her black scarf still knotted round her neck.

Close-up of the YOUNG MAN, gazing at her with amusement and admiration in his eyes, from over the top of the plumes.

Resume on the GIRL. She puts her blouse down and stands waiting. They look at each other, suddenly serious and tense.

Camera moves with THOMAS as he goes up to her, ducking under the plume rack, and places his hands on her shoulders. He looks at her silently.

Reverse angle shot of them looking at one another. He moves away and she turns to look at him.

THOMAS : *Get dressed. I'll cut out the negatives you want.*

He goes off down the gangway leading to the darkrooms. He opens the purple door of the first one.

Inside the darkroom the door slides open, revealing THOMAS in close-up. Camera follows him as he goes to the table and takes the reel from the camera. He toys with it, as if still undecided whether to give it to her or not. Then he puts it out of sight and picks up another roll of film, and turns back to the door.*

He comes back into the studio and looks round, toying with the film still in his hand. At first glance it seems the GIRL has disappeared. The music is now cool, quiet jazz.

The GIRL's legs are visible, but the rest of her body is obscured by the lilac back-drop. He pulls it away from the wall and looks behind it. She is standing still, half-naked, with her arms folded across her breasts. THOMAS comes towards her behind the purple paper, holding it back, then letting it fall, obscuring them both from view.

THOMAS comes up to the GIRL and tosses her the roll of film. She takes it and moves away, camera following her. But after one or two steps she stops and turns back. She looks at THOMAS almost tenderly. Then gives him a kiss. A fleeting kiss. And again moves away.

This time it is his turn to follow her. She stands in close-up

---

* End of reel 3.

against the purple screen, and he takes her in his arms, holds her tight and kisses her. This, too, is brief.

Then, with an arm round her shoulders, he leads her gently towards the bedroom. As they pass, camera tracks in rapidly to the GIRL's blouse as she tosses the reel of film onto it.

They reach the doorway to the bedroom. She wraps her arms round his neck . . . when the doorbell rings. They both pause.

THOMAS taking off his shirt : *They'll go.*

He tosses the shirt into the bedroom and stands bare-chested. The bell rings again.

GIRL : *But they're not going.*

The YOUNG MAN makes a move to go and open the door. But it is she who holds him back, with a hand on his shoulder.

GIRL : *Don't go.*

The YOUNG MAN gives her hand a kiss and goes down the stairs.

THOMAS crosses the receptionist's office and opens the front door. A DELIVERY BOY stands outside.

DELIVERY BOY : *Have you bought a propeller?*

THOMAS : *What?*

DELIVERY BOY : *You bought a propeller this morning. Right?*

THOMAS : *Oh, yes.*

DELIVERY BOY : *You'll have to give us a hand with it.*

THOMAS steps outside to see, then comes back inside to get the key to the big garage door from a chest of drawers in the hall. He picks it up and goes outside.

Outside in the street the DELIVERY BOY unties the propeller from the top of his van, while THOMAS unlocks the garage door.

From the platform overlooking the studio we see the two of them coming in carrying the propeller.

They put it down on the floor near the smoked glass panels.

DELIVERY BOY : *All right?*

THOMAS : *Fine. Yes.* The DELIVERY BOY goes off.

We see THOMAS's reflection in a mirror as he turns to go back to the GIRL, going up the steps.

76

GIRL off : *What's it for?*

He hurries up the narrow stairs, but she has already come out onto the platform above. She is still half-naked, with her arms folded across her body, as she bends down, looking down at the propeller.

THOMAS : *Nothing. It's beautiful.*

GIRL : *If I had a big room like this I'd hang it from the ceiling like a fan.*

THOMAS leads her back into the studio.

THOMAS : *Do you live on your own?*

Camera pans as THOMAS comes back into the studio.

GIRL off : *No.*

She follows him up the steps, ducking under the ostrich plumes. A pause. They move towards the end of the room.

THOMAS gesturing : *Perhaps I'll put it there like a piece of sculpture.*

GIRL : *It'll look good there. It'll break up the straight lines.*

THOMAS takes two cigarettes out of a packet and offers one to the GIRL, who is standing with her hands resting lightly on a beam above her head. (Still on page 59) She accepts. He gives her a light.

Now the GIRL is sitting in an armchair, still without her blouse on. She laughs, leaning back against the arm of the chair. When she leans her head forward her glance falls on the watch on her wrist. She turns serious, and gets up, hurrying off.

THOMAS off : *Are you going?*

GIRL : *It's late.*

THOMAS moves towards her.

Close-up of THOMAS as he comes up to the GIRL.

THOMAS : *Do I see you again?*

The GIRL shrugs her shoulders. She is slipping on her blouse. Again she is on edge.

THOMAS : *Well, at least tell me your name . . . your phone number.*

The GIRL looks in her bag for a piece of paper. While THOMAS is getting her one, she puts the reel into her bag.

THOMAS finds some paper and a pencil and gives them to her.

She scribbles something on the paper and starts for the door, tucking in her blouse. Halfway down the stairs she turns round and looks up.

GIRL : *Thank you*. Then she disappears.

THOMAS is alone in the studio. We see him standing at the top of the stairs. He folds the slip of paper and puts it in his pocket. We can see him, partially obscured by the ostrich plumes. He turns off the record player, pours himself another drink and sits down, tapping his knee. He sips some wine. He doesn't really know what to do. Suddenly, he puts his glass down, gets up and runs out.

THOMAS comes into the passage, and camera pans with him as he tucks in his shirt and rolls up his sleeves, going into the first darkroom. He picks up the reel exposed in the park that morning and sets it up for developing. Then he slides the door shut behind him, shutting himself in. Camera moves across the red warning light outside flashing on.

He takes the negatives out of the developing cabinet.

The door in the hall slides open and the red light flashes off. THOMAS comes out of the first darkroom and goes into the second, which has a green door. He shuts himself in, and the second red light goes on.

The negatives are placed in strips of five on a light table. THOMAS studies them through a magnifying glass. One shot in particular seems to catch his attention. He puts a pencil mark on it.

Seen in close-up, he puts the frame into the enlarger and switches off the main light and the light underneath the frosted glass, then switches on the yellow ' safe ' light.

A sheet of photographic paper is hanging on the wall. THOMAS, standing by the enlarger, presses a button : the image of the meadow on the hill-top, and the couple, is projected onto the sheet. THOMAS takes out the sheet, and submerges it in the developing tank.

Seen from the big studio below, he comes out of the darkroom with the blow-up still dripping in his hand, and camera moves back as he crosses the catwalk to the upstairs studio, leaping up the steps.

THOMAS is sitting in back view on his sofa, looking at two blow-ups hanging from the beam which runs across the studio. He lights a cigarette.

He kneels closer, staring at the prints.

Close-up of one print. In it the GIRL can be seen pulling the MAN by the arm, but they are a long way away. Camera pans across to the other, in which they are not so far away, and kissing. A sense of utter peacefulness emanates from both photographs. But the GIRL's behaviour is not entirely natural: the effort she is making to drag the MAN across to the other side of the field. And more than that, as she is embracing the MAN, she seems to be looking with a strangely tense expression at something out of the picture. Camera moves in closer and back to the first blow-up.

THOMAS gets up, and camera moves in to the blank back of the photograph. His shadow can be seen through the paper, moving about as he studies it.

Close-up of THOMAS looking at the pictures. He turns and walks off, his footsteps echoing through the empty studio.

THOMAS comes back with another blow-up, which he hangs beside the other two. He stands back, scrutinizing it. (Still on page 60)

It is a close-up enlargement of the couple embracing: the anxious expression stamped on the GIRL's face can be seen clearly as she looks over the MAN's shoulder.

Resume on THOMAS. He goes back and looks at the long shot of the photograph, to find out what might be attracting the GIRL's attention. He runs his finger along the GIRL's line of vision. But the whole meadow is surrounded by shrubbery, and at that point amongst the trees where presumably the GIRL's line of sight ends there is nothing visibly out of the ordinary. He shrugs and goes off.

THOMAS puts on a record and pours himself another drop of wine. He comes and sits down again. We can see him from between two of the blow-ups hanging on the beam. He drinks, still gazing at the photographs.

Close-up of his hand putting down his glass and picking up a magnifying glass off the glass coffee table. Camera tracks in on him as he peers through the magnifying glass at the couple embracing. The GIRL's line of sight is directed at one particular point amongst the shrubbery, and here the PHOTOGRAPHER focuses the glass. As if he had discovered something or at least had a suspicion, he draws a square with a white wax pencil around an area of vegetation. He takes the print down and moves off towards the darkroom.

THOMAS examines a new blow-up pinned to the wall — an enlargement of the area he marked.

We see the picture of the GIRL and the MAN embracing. Camera moves across to the new blow-up: amongst the vegetation a white patch can be seen — it could be a man's face emerging from the vegetation and staring. And staring directly towards the couple. Probably watching the GIRL. And she, presumably, is watching him. Camera moves back and tracks in to the picture of the couple, then moves back and tracks in even closer to the face in the bushes.

Close-up of THOMAS in back view, staring at the pictures. He backs away and looks at them all from a distance.

THOMAS is now in the darkroom again. He has all the photographs he took that morning in front of him on the counter top, enlarged to 18 by 24. He circles other particulars. (Still on page 61)

He comes back into the studio and hangs the new blow-ups on the wall. Next to the one of the man hiding in the trees, THOMAS hangs one of the GIRL, holding her hand out in front of her. (Still on page 62)

Another print shows the GIRL when she has just become aware of the PHOTOGRAPHER's presence and is looking anxiously towards him, gently disengaging herself from the MAN's embrace. Camera moves in to a third print showing the GIRL looking thoughtful, biting her fingernail, presumably intent on

80

following the PHOTOGRAPHER'S movements at the other end of the meadow. The MAN is also looking towards the PHOTO-GRAPHER attentively. Then we move on to the last blow-up, which shows the MAN still looking towards the other end of the meadow, at the point where the GIRL must have run off towards the PHOTOGRAPHER. THOMAS stands thoughtfully in front of this blow-up. Trying to collate expressions, lines of vision and situations, he pauses for a moment to think.

He leans on the arm of the sofa. Then he remembers the slip of paper on which the GIRL wrote her name and telephone number. He picks up the telephone from under the armchair, sits down and dials the number.

THOMAS : *Hello? Knightsbridge one-two-three-nine? . . .. What? . . . No, I'm sorry.*

The GIRL has given him a wrong number. THOMAS slams down the receiver and angrily tosses the slip of paper away. Then he goes back to study the blow-ups.

THOMAS comes up to two pictures : one of the GIRL at the top of the steps and one of the man in the bushes. He lingers over the latter, examining every detail. He sits down in front of it. Something in the photograph attracts his attention. Something strange enough to send him scurrying off once more in the direction of the darkroom.

THOMAS is in the darkroom, lifting the new blow-up out of the washing tray and examining it closely.

He comes back into the studio and pins the blow-up to the wall. It is an enlargement of the man hiding; he is holding a pistol. THOMAS removes the one of the GIRL on the steps.

THOMAS is standing on the sofa to pin up the picture. (Still on page 62) He takes the GIRL'S photograph and pins it on a beam on the other side of the room. By arranging the blow-ups in sequence along the walls, THOMAS has succeeded in recon-structing the whole episode.

We see all the photographs in a series of close-ups. The first photograph is the long shot in which the GIRL is pulling the MAN by the arm.

An enlargement of the couple from the same picture.

The third is another long shot with the two of them embracing. Then the close-up of the couple. The GIRL is looking across at a particular point in the clump of trees. Camera moves across the picture, following the GIRL's line of vision to the point in the clump of trees where there is an indistinct light patch, perhaps a man hiding amongst the trees.

The patch blown up. It is obviously a man.

The detail of the man's hand holding a pistol fitted with telescopic sights and silencer.

The GIRL, still in the MAN's arms, seeing the PHOTOGRAPHER for the first time.

The GIRL and the MAN. Both are looking in the direction of the PHOTOGRAPHER.

The MAN on his own, looking fairly agitated but not as much as his companion.

The GIRL in close-up watching the PHOTOGRAPHER, biting her nail in anxiety.

The GIRL, coming up to the PHOTOGRAPHER, covering her face with her hand so as not to be recognizable in the photograph.

The GIRL standing still near a clump of bushes on the other side of the meadow.

An enlargement of the GIRL. Her expression suggests she is witnessing something unusual.

The empty meadow.

Camera moves in and round past the last two blow-ups to focus on THOMAS, in close-up, meditating on the story he has edited together. (Still on page 62) He cannot help but feel a certain satisfaction. Camera moves with him as he reaches for the telephone and dials a number.

THOMAS : *Ron? . . . Something fantastic's happened. Those photographs in the park . . . fantastic . . . Somebody was trying to kill somebody else. I saved his life . . . Listen, Ron, there — there was a girl . . . Ron, will you listen! What makes it so fantastic . . .*

The front door bell rings.

THOMAS : *Look, hang on, will you, Ron? There's somebody at the door.*

Close-up of one of the pictures of the GIRL and the MAN. THOMAS's gaze falls on it as he passes on his way to the door. He looks at it as if hoping the GIRL were the one ringing the bell.

He crosses the receptionist's office, then stands for a moment looking perplexed in front of the closed door. Slowly he lets it open, standing behind it. A girl is pushed inside backwards, then hurries out at once. In her place appears the young BLONDE who had turned up in the morning, wanting to be photographed. THOMAS is rather taken aback, and obviously disappointed.

BLONDE : *You weren't expecting us, were you?*

THOMAS : *No.*

With a curt nod he invites them in. The BLONDE rushes inside, followed quickly by her brunette friend. Camera moves with her, then down to reveal her red tights and then her friend's green tights. Once inside, they turn to look at THOMAS as he closes the door. Another nod from THOMAS, meaning they should follow him.

The two girls run giggling up the stairs.

THOMAS off : *Could you manage to make a cup of coffee between you?*

They stop and lean over the bannisters, looking down at him. (Still on page 63)

BLONDE : *I can make an Irish coffee, if you like . . .* They both giggle.

Close-up of THOMAS coming up the stairs. As he reaches the girls they all start climbing. They hesitate before going into the kitchen.

THOMAS : *All right, come on.*

In the kitchen, they go on giggling, almost by force of habit. THOMAS gets out the tin of coffee and the percolator, and hands everything to the BRUNETTE. Then he takes down two coffee cups and turns again towards the BLONDE, saying :

87

THOMAS : *Is she always like that?*
BLONDE : *Like what?*
THOMAS : *Doesn't speak.*

He goes up to the BRUNETTE, and pokes his face into hers.

THOMAS : *What's your name?* He breaks off, moving away again.
Ah, forget it. What's the use of a name? What do they call you in bed?

The BLONDE starts giggling again.

Close-up of the BRUNETTE, who says in a sulky voice :

BRUNETTE : *I only go to bed to sleep.*

THOMAS starts circling her and staring as if she were a rare specimen of the animal world. He stops near the BLONDE, pointing his thumb at her friend, and seems about to say something concerning her. But suddenly he remembers that he left RON on the telephone and hurries off into the studio, handing the BLONDE the cups. The BLONDE whispers to her friend.

BLONDE : *What should I have . . . ?* But the BRUNETTE puts her finger to her lips, telling her to be quiet. Both listen to THOMAS in the other room shouting down the telephone.

THOMAS off : *Hello! . . .*

Medium shot of THOMAS sitting on the edge of the armchair holding the telephone in his hand. Getting no reply, he dials the number again.

THOMAS : *Hello?*

From the doorway of the dressing room, adjacent to the kitchen, the BRUNETTE hisses to her friend to come in.

BRUNETTE : *Psst. Look at all these clothes!*

They both go into the dressing room, camera following them. They start rummaging through the dresses hanging from a long clothes rack. The BRUNETTE picks one out and holds it up.

BRUNETTE : *Oooh . . .*

The BLONDE looks up. She doesn't like it.

BLONDE : *No!*

Her friend puts it back on the rack. She chooses another. The BLONDE does the same.

BLONDE : *Hey, how about this one?*
BRUNETTE : *Put it on.*

The BRUNETTE helps the other girl out of her dress. The BLONDE is bare-topped, with nothing on but her green tights pulled up to her waist.

The BLONDE is just slipping into the dress when THOMAS appears in the doorway, startling the girls.

BRUNETTE : *Oh!*

THOMAS turns to her; she is still fully dressed.

THOMAS : *What about you? Help yourself!*

The coffee pot has started whistling from the kitchen. The BRUNETTE seizes her opportunity.

BRUNETTE : *The coffee!*

She rushes into the kitchen to take the coffee off the stove.

Close-up of the BLONDE. THOMAS's hand grabs the strap of her dress and pulls it off again. She quickly covers her nudity with her own dress which is draped over the rack; she is a little frightened, and ducks behind the clothes rack. THOMAS pulls the rack away.

The rack falls on the floor, revealing the girl pressed against the wall clutching her dress to her breasts.

THOMAS reaches for her dress. He pulls her towards him (Still on page 63), and pulls it away from her, tossing it onto the floor. Then he pulls her long blonde hair across her face, and takes hold of her hand and arm, trying to pull her towards him. The BLONDE screams and tries to free herself.

Close-up of the BLONDE biting him on the hand. They start struggling and he throws her roughly onto the floor.

The BRUNETTE appears on the threshold.

BRUNETTE : *What's the matter?*

The BLONDE gets to her feet. She is in a wild mood and laughs madly, pointing at her friend.

BLONDE : *She's got a better figure than me.*

BRUNETTE : *Oh, it's not true!*

THOMAS and the BLONDE try to catch the BRUNETTE, who edges towards the door.

Close-up of Thomas blocking the doorway and pushing the girls into the room.

Girls : *Oh no! Ohhh* . . .

Thomas stands with his back to the wall, grinning. Camera moves down with the Blonde, who throws her arms round her friend and drags her onto the floor. Both are laughing and squealing and fighting on the pile of dresses. The Blonde is going wild, and tries to rip off her friend's dress. She manages to undo the zip.

Close-up of Thomas laughing.

Thomas crouches, watching the girls, laughing and urging them on.

Thomas : *Go on, practise. Go on! Give her a left hook!*

The two girls roll across the floor amongst the clothes, laughing and screaming uncontrollably.

Thomas off : *I'll put you in a ring together* . . .

The girls struggle on the floor, still laughing. It is a mock fight, playful and exciting.

Thomas watches their antics with amusement. (Stills on pages 63 and 64)

Close-up of the Blonde and her friend. The Blonde is tenacious in her efforts to strip the other girl, and at last removes her dress. Then they both scramble to their feet.

Thomas stands up as the two girls run out towards the studio. He follows them.*

The Blonde chases the Brunette into the studio, both clad only in tights. Camera moves in as the Brunette hides behind the back-drop of lilac paper. She is holding a red dress protectively against her naked body.

Camera pans with the Brunette as the Blonde grabs the mauve back-drop and begins to tear it down.

Resume on the Brunette as her friend hauls on the huge roll of paper.

Close-up of the Blonde unrolling the back-drop completely.

---

* End of reel 4.

The BLONDE laughs triumphantly as the BRUNETTE appears holding up part of the back-drop against her chest.

Close-up of them as the BLONDE grabs the BRUNETTE and they fall onto the folds of back-drop paper. (Still on page 81)

THOMAS catches up with them and laughingly enters the fray.

Close-up of THOMAS on the floor with the girls, pulling off the BLONDE's tights.

THOMAS half-rises and tugs at the BLONDE's tights, as she giggles helplessly. The BRUNETTE helps.

BRUNETTE : *Hold her legs!*

Close-up of them all. THOMAS tugs at the BLONDE's tights; she offers no resistance. The BRUNETTE still makes some effort to cover herself with the back-drop paper.

The back-drop tears and collapses in the foreground, revealing THOMAS. He gets the BLONDE's tights off and hangs them round his neck, and then she crawls gleefully across to the BRUNETTE, pulling at her tights.

Close-up of the BLONDE pulling the BRUNETTE's tights off, assisted by THOMAS.

The BLONDE holds her friend down while THOMAS pulls the tights from her kicking legs.

Close-up of the two girls laughing hilariously as THOMAS removes the BRUNETTE's tights completely.

The girls are now naked. The BLONDE drags THOMAS down with her onto the floor and rolls on top of him, their laughter and shouting smothered every now and then by the paper. The BRUNETTE sits watching, covering herself with the purple paper. As THOMAS struggles with the BLONDE, she tears off his shirt, then clutches at his belt. The BRUNETTE throws off all pretence at modesty and helps by holding him down. We leave the three of them screaming and laughing.

Some time has passed. It is very quiet. Camera tilts down from the plastic window to THOMAS — lying flat on his back on the floor, his chest bare. The two girls are now dressed again, and are putting his socks on, each one holding a foot. THOMAS raises his head : something outside the field of vision has attracted his attention. (Still on page 81) Slowly he gets to his feet.

Close-up of THOMAS, his eyes riveted to this something. The BLONDE passes him his shirt. THOMAS snatches it and slips it on as he moves away, leaving her standing puzzled.

The photographs hang in the foreground. THOMAS comes forward, examining them closely. A horrible thought seems to cross his mind. Camera tracks with him, then pans down to the BRUNETTE sitting on the floor, looking puzzled.

Close-up of THOMAS. He looks at the last photograph through the magnifying glass. (Still on page 81) Then he studies the picture of the GIRL walking away, holding the glass to her legs. He is studying a spot on both photographs where a dark patch is visible on the ground, quite near the bushes.

THOMAS turns suddenly, hurrying towards the darkroom. But he remembers the two girls, who are standing waiting expectantly behind him.

THOMAS curtly : *All right, let's move. Out!*

BLONDE : *You haven't taken any photographs!*

THOMAS : *No, I'm . . . No, I'm too whacked. Well, it's your own faults.*

The two girls look at each other in disappointment. THOMAS motions for them to put on their shoes. Camera tilts down and then up as they do as they are told, and start moving off.

THOMAS : *Tomorrow.*

The BLONDE and the BRUNETTE hesitate in the kitchen doorway and turn once more to the PHOTOGRAPHER. He shouts at them :

THOMAS : *Tomorrow!*

The two girls disappear.

Close-up of THOMAS. He runs his hand over his head, lost in thought for a moment. Then he makes for the darkrooms.

He is seen through the plastic window as he walks towards the narrow catwalk, slowly, hesitantly, as if again oppressed by his fearful suspicions.

He comes into the last darkroom with the large blow-up of the

GIRL standing by the bush already completed. He tacks it to a wooden panel, then directs the light from two projectors onto it. He moves a large plate camera, setting the distance so that the small dark patch will be greatly enlarged. He takes a time exposure (Still on page 82), then goes out of the room with the photographic plate in his hand.

In another darkroom he draws a new huge blow-up out of the dryer.

He comes into the studio with this blow-up and sticks it up on the plume stand where he has already placed the first blow-up of the empty meadow.

Close-up of THOMAS. He moves away, and camera tracks in on the two pictures, first to one then to the other, then back to the first. Both pictures suggest that the patch by the bushes at the GIRL's feet is a corpse stretched out on the grass.

Close-up of THOMAS staring at the pictures. He runs his fingers nervously through his hair, and goes to have another look at the photograph of the man hiding in the trees with the pistol in his hand. Camera follows him as he drops back onto the sofa and lies back.

THOMAS sits, confused, on the sofa. He looks up at the photographs on the wall behind him. He seems depressed and more disconcerted than ever. But suddenly he springs to his feet and goes out, spurred by a new idea.

Outside. It is night. The Rolls-Royce emerges from the narrow street past the antique shop and pulls up near the park entrance. The headlights go off, then THOMAS jumps out and hurries forward across the road.

He comes into the park, and camera follows him, holding on the great neon sign on the nearby rise which emits a garish light. (Still on page 83) THOMAS hurries on.

The park is deserted, silent, dark. Only the leaves rustle faintly in the breeze. THOMAS comes up the steps into the meadow, and camera moves back in front of him. He quickens his pace. He comes to the meadow. The light of the neon sign barely shows his path. He breaks into a run.

THOMAS hurries forward, then slows down, hesitantly, as he nears the bushes.

Close-up of THOMAS. Camera moves in on him as he stops suddenly, then it tilts down, revealing the ghastly white face of a dead man, his eyes still open. It is the GIRL's companion.

THOMAS steps forward. He looks round nervously as camera moves across to the rustling bushes. Then down as he stoops over the corpse.

Close-up of THOMAS. His eyes betray his awareness of the gravity of the event rather than panic or terror.

Close-up of the dead man, his face stiffened in the same, diffident, ambiguous expression which THOMAS had seen in the morning, when he was still alive, strolling there with the GIRL. THOMAS rises very slowly.

Close-up of THOMAS. A sound like a twig snapping makes him whip round. He peers in amongst the trees, where the murderer stood that morning. The impenetrable darkness, that could still be hiding someone, sends a chill down his spine.

Another, fainter sound. THOMAS moves, looking cautiously all around. The light from the neon sign silhouettes him and the figure on the grass. (Still on page 83) He sets off at a run towards the path leading to the exit, turning back from time to time to see if someone — the murderer perhaps — is not following him.[4]

THOMAS arrives back in the studio and walks slowly across the vast ground floor room, seen through the smoked glass panels, stopping by the propeller on the floor. He prods it with his foot. He moves towards the staircase and stands reflected in the large mirror there (Still on page 83), then changes his mind. He reaches the small door at the farther end of the room.

THOMAS comes out into the yard, and camera follows him as he walks across.

THOMAS is seen in close-up as he crosses the yard to BILL's house. As usual, the door is ajar. THOMAS lets himself in.

The light is on in the corridor but the house seems to be empty.

A radio is playing a piano solo. THOMAS comes forward, then stops and turns, hearing a sound.

Through the venetian blinds we see him move towards the bedroom door and stand outside looking in, struck by what he sees.

[BILL and PATRICIA are in bed making love, seen through the door. Their heavy breathing can be heard above the piano solo coming over the radio.

THOMAS looks at them, slightly startled.

Close-up of PATRICIA. She catches sight of THOMAS and stares at him, her head thrown back over the edge of the bed. BILL is oblivious to his presence.]*

THOMAS is about to withdraw discreetly.

Resume on BILL and PATRICIA. She shakes her head, in a desperate attempt to restrain THOMAS.

Close-up of PATRICIA. She nods towards THOMAS, in her eyes a clear invitation to stay.

THOMAS comes back, but he is ill at ease.

[Close-up of PATRICIA smiling. She stares at THOMAS right until the orgasm, as if the man who is on top of her were excluded from the act, and instead it was THOMAS exciting her.

THOMAS turns away, tearing his eyes from the couple.

The sink is full of dirty dishes.

THOMAS turns back, but keeps his head lowered.

PATRICIA, seen in close-up, stares at him imploringly.

THOMAS looks for something else on which to fix his attention.]*

The ashtray on the table is full of butts; the radio is beside it.

The bedclothes move, then camera moves away to one of BILL'S paintings on the wall above the bed.

Resume on BILL and PATRICIA. Camera tracks out as THOMAS passes behind the venetian blinds and hurries out of the house. BILL raises his head at the sound of the door closing.

THOMAS comes up the stairs in his house and goes into the

* The sections in square brackets were cut from the version of the film released in the U.S.A.

studio. The purple paper lies crumpled in a heap in the foreground.

THOMAS looks around. Something strikes him immediately.

The whole studio is revealed. It takes only a moment to realize that the photographs have gone from the walls and rafters.

THOMAS stands perplexed. Camera moves on past him to the living area.

THOMAS stands there as if lost in a bad dream; he lowers his head.

Close-up of THOMAS's reflection in the glass coffee table.

THOMAS starts looking around. Suddenly he remembers the roll of negatives.

He looks in the film storage cabinet. Then camera moves with him as he hurries across the catwalk.

Close-up of THOMAS sliding open the first darkroom door. It is in a mess. But the negatives are not there. He goes into the second darkroom.

In here THOMAS searches through all the cabinets. Everything has been overturned and not a trace of the negatives remains. He taps his hand on the counter top, thinking.

Then goes back into the studio in consternation. It is obvious that the murderers have taken away the only tangible evidence of what had happened. As he looks around he comes across just one of the blow-ups, between the two film storage cabinets. Close-up of the photograph. It seems to be just a random jumble of black and white dots, but it is in fact the extreme close-up of the corpse. This blow-up is the one piece of concrete evidence left in the place of the sequence of real events which he had inadvertently witnessed and recorded earlier. But even this blow-up seems now utterly meaningless.

Close-up of THOMAS. He leans forward to see the picture better when the sound of footsteps frightens him. He jerks his head up: they are coming closer, up the wooden staircase. THOMAS scurries into a hiding-place.

The slender figure of a woman appears at the top of the stairs. It is PATRICIA. She smiles at THOMAS.

PATRICIA in a perfectly natural voice : *Were you looking for something just now?*

Close-up of THOMAS. Rather at a loss for words, he stares at her face, as if looking for some indication as to how he should answer.

THOMAS : *No.*

PATRICIA off : *Oh.*

THOMAS goes up to her.

THOMAS : *Do you ever think of leaving him?*

PATRICIA : *No, I don't think so.*

THOMAS looks at her closely. PATRICIA is a little embarrassed, and turns away. A long pause. It is as if THOMAS would like to ask her something else, but suddenly it becomes impossible for him to put it into words. Then THOMAS speaks again, in a very different tone :

THOMAS : *I saw a man killed this morning.*

PATRICIA turning back towards him : *Where?*

THOMAS : *Shot. In some sort of park.*

A corner of one of the photographs is still pinned up to a beam. He pulls it down and studies it.

PATRICIA : *Are you sure?*

THOMAS : *He's still there.*

PATRICIA takes a few steps towards him.

PATRICIA : *Who was he?*

Close-up of the two of them.

THOMAS : *Someone.*

Another close-up from reverse angle. PATRICIA is watching him a little incredulously.

PATRICIA : *How did it happen?*

THOMAS : *I don't know. I didn't see.*

She moves closer and stares at him.

PATRICIA : *You didn't see.*

The YOUNG MAN is slightly ashamed.

THOMAS murmuring apologetically : *No.*

PATRICIA : *Shouldn't you call the police?*

THOMAS ignores this advice. He nods towards the photograph

97

of the dead man, on the floor.

THOMAS : *That's the body.*

PATRICIA bends down, picks up the blow-up and studies it. Then she turns to THOMAS again, with an uncertain smile, betraying her doubts as to whether he really means what he is saying.

PATRICIA : *It looks like one of Bill's paintings.*

For the first time THOMAS seems to notice it too.

THOMAS : *Yes.*

The mention of BILL's name seems to compel them to consider the strange situation they are in. PATRICIA puts down the photograph. She wanders about a bit, deep in thought, then again she turns to THOMAS.

PATRICIA : *Will you help me?*

Close-up of THOMAS, seen over PATRICIA's shoulder. She seems distraught.

PATRICIA : *I don't know what to do.*

Resume on PATRICIA. THOMAS draws near her. He watches her, perhaps for the first time trying to fathom what it might be that is disturbing her.

THOMAS : *What is it? Huh?*

A pause. PATRICIA moves away.

Resume on THOMAS, with PATRICIA standing a little way away from him. She moves away, glancing at the fragment of photographic paper.

PATRICIA : *I wonder why they shot him . . .*

She turns towards him.

Close-up of THOMAS. He leans back, looking at her.

Close-up of PATRICIA. She lowers her eyes.

Resume on the two of them. THOMAS puts the torn corner of the photograph on the cabinet behind him.

THOMAS : *I didn't ask.*

Close-up of PATRICIA. Camera follows her as she starts to go out, then stops again under the ostrich plumes as if to say something. But she just smiles at him and walks down the stairs.

THOMAS stands there lost in thought as the sound of PATRICIA's footsteps recedes.

THOMAS crosses his arms over his chest, trying to decide what to do.[5] Then suddenly he rushes forward to the telephone and dials a number.

THOMAS : *Hello, Ron? . . . Oh, hello, love, is Ron there? . . . No, I just wanted to take him somewhere. Where is he? . . . Okay. I'll fetch him there. Bye-bye, love.*

He puts down the receiver and hurries off.*

The Rolls-Royce is cruising through a street in central London.[6] THOMAS glances over at some shop windows, which are brightly lit, and then brakes violently, pulling up at the kerb.

Close-up of THOMAS, staring intently at something over his shoulder.

A small crowd of people stand in front of one of the shop windows. Among them is the GIRL from the park.

Close-up of THOMAS. He starts to get out, looking round to make sure that she is still there.

Other pedestrians pass in front of the crowd looking round the shop window. The GIRL turns and disappears into the milling throng of people. THOMAS jumps out of the car and rushes up, but the GIRL is no longer there.

We follow THOMAS as he runs in and out among the people wandering along the pavement.

THOMAS stops and looks about as people pass to and fro along the pavement. The group of people behind whom the GIRL seemed to be hiding has dispersed, and now there is no one in front of the shop window. She has completely disappeared. THOMAS runs to the end of an alley, looking for her, but it is deserted. He looks round in all directions. Nothing. He sees another alley leading off the main street a little farther back.

He tries there next, and runs down the whole length of the dark and narrow street. At the end he comes into a courtyard : this too is deserted.

---

* End of reel 5.

Strains of music come floating out of the door of a club. THOMAS goes up a short flight of iron steps and pushes the door open.

He walks along the corridor to the club. Signs on the door read:

HERE LIES	I LOVE
BOB	HAROLD
DYLAN	
PASSED AWAY	
ROYAL ALBERT	IT WAS EITHER
HALL 27 MAY	THIS OR
1966	A MILK ROUND
R.I.P.	

Posters all along the wall advertise forthcoming fixtures.
He goes inside.

It is a very dim but spacious room, with great white portraits of rock stars painted on the black walls. The place is full of young people. We follow THOMAS as he moves among them, looking for the GIRL. A group, the Yardbirds, is playing up on stage. The music is deafening.

SINGER singing off: *Stroll on*
        'Cause . . .

THOMAS moves through the crowd looking for the GIRL. Nobody takes any notice of him. They are all listening to the music, keeping absolutely still, not even following the rhythm by moving their heads, their hands or feet. The Yardbirds continue their number.

SINGER: . . . *it's all gone*
       Treat you right
       You make me cry
       You're tellin' me
       You didn't see . . .

Close-up of THOMAS in the crowd.

SINGER off: *I love no more*
       If you wanna know

100

I love you so . . .

Another close-up of THOMAS, still searching the faces in the crowd.

SINGER off : . . . *And I don't wanna let you go*
   Stroll on
   Stroll with your feet
   Stroll . . .

Resume on the Yardbirds, watched by the crowd of young people.

Camera pans with THOMAS pushing his way round.

SINGER off : . . . *on*
   'Cause you really love me
   Stroll on
   Be a pair tonight
   Stroll on . . .

Close-up of the lead guitarist.

SINGER off : . . . *It'll be your turn tonight*
   If you don't change your mind . . .

Resume on the group, seen from below.

SINGER : . . . *You ain't gonna find anymore my kind . . .*

Resume on the lead guitarist, playing a solo.

THOMAS edges through the crowd. As he passes, camera follows him revealing the only couple dancing : a blonde girl wearing striped trousers and a silver coat and a West Indian in maroon trousers.

Behind the two dancers, THOMAS goes and looks among some people sitting on chairs lined up against the wall, listening. The GIRL is not there.

THOMAS moves behind another group of listeners.

He moves towards another group, looking around. Camera follows his zigzag movements through the audience thronged round the stage. THOMAS moves through the crowd right by the stage.

The group can be seen from the back of the stage. The crowd watches silently below them. But there is something wrong with one of the loudspeakers : it begins to crackle. The lead

101

guitarist shows signs of nervousness and stops playing for a moment. He and the singer try to adjust the speaker. Then he continues playing, and the singer moves away.

The lead guitarist continues to play but he is still having trouble. He fiddles with the control knob and the singer comes across to help. He adjusts something at the back of the speaker. The crowd watch interestedly as the lead guitarist comes back to the edge of the stage and starts to play again. But the loudspeaker is still playing up. The guitarist is getting more and more edgy — finally he turns and smashes his guitar against the offending speaker, without ceasing to play.

SINGER off : . . . *Stroll on . . .*

> *. . . The reason why*
> *You make me cry . . .*

The spectators seem to be fascinated by this development. Even THOMAS breaks off his search to see what is happening.

SINGER off : . . . *You didn't see*

> *A richer beau*
> *I love her no more . . .*

The guitarist again bangs the speaker with his guitar, watched by the crowd who stand facing him in the background.

SINGER off : . . . *Do you wanna know*

> *I love you so*
> *I don't wanna let you go*
> *Stroll . . .*

The guitarist hits the loudspeaker again, as a boy hurries onto the stage from the crowd, flipping buttons on the amplification control box, gesturing at the guitarist.

SINGER off : . . . *on*

> *Gonna make you see*
> *Stroll on*
> *'Cause you really love me*
> *Stroll on*
> *It'll be your turn tonight*
> *Stroll on . . .*

The guitarist stands in front of the boy trying to fix the

102

amplifier. The singer continues his song accompanied by the remaining members of the group.

SINGER : . . . *If you don't change your mind*
You ain't gonna find anymore my kind . . .

The guitarist turns and hits the guitar against the amplifier with renewed strength. He is banging the neck of his guitar so hard against the loudspeaker that the instrument shatters.

He throws it viciously on the floor.

GUITARIST, to the SINGER : *Give 'em the song again.*

Close-up of the guitarist's foot stamping on the guitar, going right through.

We see another member of the group playing bass guitar, then camera moves across to the singer.

SINGER : . . . *Stroll on*
'Cause it's all gone
Treat you right . . .

The drummer plays furiously, keeping up an insistent rhythm.

SINGER off : . . . *You make me cry*
You're tellin' me . . .

Close-up of the lead guitarist kneeling down by his guitar. By now it is split in two, and only held together by the strings. He snaps these as well. Then he picks up the neck of the shattered guitar and starts to throw it into the audience.

SINGER off : . . . *You didn't see . . .*
. . . I love no more
If you wanna know I love you so . . .

At this, all hell breaks loose. Everyone in the audience wants that piece of guitar. From the stage, we see them scream and push, and some end up on the floor.

Camera pans down to a group of girls fighting over the fragment.

Close-up of the singer. Girls in the audience scream hysterically as he finishes the song for the second time.

SINGER : . . . *If you don't change your mind*
You ain't gonna find anymore my kind.

Even THOMAS gets caught up in the scuffle : in fact he is

103

perhaps the wildest of them all. At the end he is the one left holding the piece of guitar. Clutching it in his hand, he shoulders his way through the crowd.

Camera pans right over the screaming crowd as THOMAS runs towards the exit.

THOMAS runs out into the passage leading to the club, pursued by the crowd.

Two girls jump aside as THOMAS rushes past, followed by two boys. One of the boys trips and falls.

THOMAS rushes out of the club, and down the alley outside.

THOMAS runs out into the main street and stops by a shop window, panting. He looks down.

Realizing that he is still clutching the piece of guitar, he tosses it away and looks around.

THOMAS rushes off in the direction of his car. A passer-by moves across and picks up the piece of guitar curiously, then throws it away again.

It is later in the evening. THOMAS comes up to the high, wrought-iron gates leading into the front garden of a house on the Chelsea embankment. He moves towards the door, and the gate swings closed behind him.

Close-up of THOMAS at the front door. He rings the front door bell.

A man opens the door and THOMAS comes into a large room full of young people. A party is in progress. Smoking, drinking, talking. There is a lively but discreet buzz in the air, and the place has an elegance of its own. THOMAS greets a couple of friends and looks around, trying to locate someone. He reaches the farther end of the room, where there are fewer people. Here a doorway leads into a bedroom across a hallway.

THOMAS comes into this room and pauses to have a look around. There are about a dozen people, sprawled on settees or on the floor. They are all smoking. Some of them pass a cigarette from hand to hand, as do people who enjoy their marijuana puff.

THOMAS stands looking round.

A group of men and girls draw on the joints, giggling gently among themselves.

One of the girls is drawing on a pipe instead of a rolled cigarette. Camera pans from her to the rest of the group. Another girl is rolling the joints, taking the marijuana out of a little bag and delicately licking the glued edge of the cigarette papers. The atmosphere is not heavy. On the contrary it is somewhat dreamlike. There is something eerie about the peace pervading the room which gives it an air of unreality.

A girl takes a long drag on a joint.

Close-up of one of the young men, smoking. Camera moves across to the girl looking down, watching him.

Another boy gets up, and camera follows him as he gives a joint to someone else. We see THOMAS picking his way through the room.

A man is kneeling in front of two girls, with his back to us. THOMAS comes over and taps him on the shoulder. As he gets up we see that it is RON.

THOMAS : *Ron. Gimme a minute, will you?*

RON gets up. He is stoned. He is smoking from two joints at once. THOMAS tries again :

THOMAS : *Ron.*

Close-up of the two girls. RON leans down to them and very slowly puts a joint in each of their mouths. He rises as THOMAS takes hold of his coat and pulls him away towards the door.

THOMAS leads RON through the hallway into a quiet corner of the main room.

THOMAS : *Someone's been killed!*

RON literally drops into an armchair, next to a girl. She goes away.

RON : *Yeah. Okay. Okay.*

THOMAS leans over him.

THOMAS : *Listen.*

A medium shot of RON and THOMAS.

THOMAS : *Those pictures I took in the park . . .*

But RON is not listening. He has turned back to the room from which they came and is signalling to someone.

It is the MODEL whom THOMAS had photographed alone in his studio that morning. The MODEL comes forward with a joint hanging out of her mouth. RON takes it from her. In the meantime THOMAS turns towards her.

THOMAS : *I thought you were supposed to be in Paris?*

MODEL : *I am in Paris.*

Close-up of RON drawing hard on the joint, forcing the smoke down into his lungs.

RON's hand passes THOMAS the joint.

Close-up of THOMAS and the MODEL.

RON off : *Here, have a drag.*

THOMAS takes it and passes it on mechanically to the MODEL, who puts it in her mouth and goes off. (Still on page 86)

THOMAS turns back to RON. He sits down in the armchair facing him, and carries on :

THOMAS : *I want you to see the corpse. We've got to get a shot of it.*

RON : *I'm not a photographer.*

THOMAS : *I am!*

THOMAS looks away from his friend, impatiently. He gets up and walks off.

Close-up of THOMAS. He looks round towards RON.

RON is slumped in the armchair.

Resume on THOMAS. He is bitterly disappointed.

Resume on RON in the chair, shaking his head uncomprehendingly. Then he gets up, muttering to himself :

RON : *What's the matter with him?*

He makes for the room where they are all smoking, as if THOMAS was not there. As he passes him, he stops, as if suddenly recalling, and looks him in the eye.

RON : *What did you see in that park?*

THOMAS looks away and shakes his head hopelessly.

THOMAS : *Nothing.*

RON goes off. THOMAS trails after him with an expression almost of dismay.

THOMAS : *Ron!*

RON has already reached the hall between the two rooms. He turns, and beckons THOMAS to follow him. As he doesn't move, RON goes back, grips him by the shoulder and leads him through to the room at the back.

RON and THOMAS disappear through the door into the other room. One of the girls comes out of the same door. She is wearing a white jacket and a long white skirt, and is still smoking a joint. She comes into the living room into the buzz of voices, and the door shuts behind her. The buzz is getting fainter and fainter. Finally there is silence.

It is dawn. In the bedroom THOMAS is stretched out asleep on the bed in the middle of the room. A pale light filters through the window. The floor is littered with ashtrays, glasses and bottles. THOMAS wakes up. He looks around, dazed, sighing deeply and rubbing his head. He glances over at the window.

THOMAS sits up. Through the windows in the background we can see trees, the roof of a house, a patch of blue sky. He gets up and leaves the room, rubbing his aching head.

THOMAS comes through the connecting hall into the living room. Here is the same confusion — glasses and bottles on tables, furniture all over the place, cushions on the floor. The River Thames is just visible through the window. Few sounds break the silence. The house is empty. THOMAS pauses for a moment to look outside, then he makes for the door. Camera holds for a few moments on the dim empty room and the river scene visible through the window. Nothing moves.

THOMAS has come back into the park again. We can see him going up the path that leads to the meadow on the hill-top. A strong, constant breeze rustles the leaves of the trees and bushes.

He retraces his steps across the meadow in the dawn-quiet park. The only sound is the wind in the trees.

THOMAS has his camera with him as usual and as he walks away towards the clump of bushes at the far end of the meadow he adjusts it, making it ready to photograph the corpse.

He comes forward, running a few steps. As he gradually comes closer to the bushes in the foreground he slows down and concentrates.

THOMAS is partly obscured by the foliage as he comes round the clump of bushes. His tension grows. He has the impression that, behind the bush, something has changed . . .

He comes right round, looking down. Camera tracks in to close-up as he stops, drawing in his breath. Could it be the wrong bush? No, it is this one, undoubtedly. But the corpse is no longer there.

THOMAS kneels down to look at the grass. He looks for any marks which the body might have left where it was stretched out.

Close-up of THOMAS from above looking at the grass. It looks perfectly normal. Hardly a blade is bent. He looks up into the sky: the wind has risen and is rustling the leaves more insistently.

The boughs which had spread above the dead man's head are moved by a stronger gust of wind. Camera tilts down from them to THOMAS. He looks down to the spot where the corpse should be, then turns and takes a few steps forward. Then he stops. Above the line of trees behind him the great neon sign looms up into the lightening sky.

From THOMAS's point of view we see part of the meadow with its border of trees. It is completely deserted.

Resume on THOMAS. He looks down to where the body lay, then across to the bottom of the meadow where another path begins, then back to the bushes. Perhaps the body has been dragged that way. But nothing. Not a trace. The huge neon sign goes out. The daylight is strengthening. THOMAS looks towards the sign and then back down to the grass under the bushes.

THOMAS stands disconsolately in front of the bushes. Then he moves off towards the path he came up by. His steps are slow, his camera dangling by his side.

In the lower part of the park a jeep is careering round the asphalt path which surrounds the field where the tennis courts are situated. It is packed with students : the same students who had been collecting money on the previous morning in the centre of London.

The jeep lurches along. The students — some hanging on for dear life — are yelling and banging their collection tins on the body of the jeep, and the noise is deafening.

Camera moves back in front of the speeding jeep.

Camera follows the jeep as it roars along behind the tennis court wire-netting.

THOMAS comes down the steps from the meadow and sees the jeep as it careers along the path below him.

Camera follows the jeep as it speeds away to the far end of the meadow.

THOMAS walks forward along the path, watching the students in the jeep.

The jeep drives behind the tennis court along the path immediately below the row of white painted houses.

THOMAS walks on over the grass as the jeep returns, the students shouting as they approach. Camera moves with the jeep as it pulls up in front of the entrance to one of the tennis courts.

The students get out, and two of them, a boy and a girl, take over one of the courts, while the others spread out along the wire-netting on the near side of the court. The students look like clowns — they are dressed in bizarre clothes and their faces are covered with white powder.

The boy on the court is wearing dungarees, and the girl wears a striped dress over black tights. They pick up balls and bounce them on their tennis racquets as they move to either end of the court and begin the game. That is to say, they mime the actions and gestures appropriate to the game. (Still on page 84) In reality they have neither racquets nor balls. However, the imaginary game gets under way, with the two players rushing around the court with convincing vigour and tenacity, but without uttering a sound.

The boy plays a forehand stroke to the girl, then runs in to take her return. But he misses the ball and gestures angrily.

Meanwhile THOMAS has moved up close to one of the corners of the court at the girl's end. He leans against the wire-netting and watches.

The players run about to hit the non-existent ball, forehands following backhands in quick succession. They even miss their shots sometimes, scolding themselves and looking mortified when they do. All of this is seen from THOMAS's viewpoint.

Their friends, who are watching outside the court, follow the game with well-simulated interest, moving their heads rhythmically, as though following the ball from one side of the net to the other. Left, right. Left, right. They stand in complete silence.

Three of the students watch silently : left, right; left, right.

A girl in a bowler hat with white spots painted on it peers through the netting, her eyes moving steadily right to left, left to right, following an imaginary rally.

Another girl looks through the netting towards the right.

Camera follows the girl playing as she runs back and ' hits ' the ball.

The boy runs forward and returns the shot vigorously.

Some of the students jump back as if the imaginary ball has hit the netting forcefully in front of them.

The boy runs off to the right after the ball.

Close-up of THOMAS watching the game. (Still on page 88) He smiles slightly.

At this point the girl misses a shot and the imaginary ball hits the back netting near THOMAS. She runs over and picks up the ball, camera following her movements. She glances at THOMAS with a shrug, as if to say : ' I missed it — it happens to us all.' She stands in the foreground, watched by THOMAS outside the netting. Then she hurries away and THOMAS smiles : he is starting to enjoy the game.

110

Things are becoming more exciting as the players start alternating smashes and volleys. The girl serves — camera follows the arc of the ball over the net to the boy, and then back; she returns with a high lob, and camera moves up and down to indicate its path. The boy smashes it back.

Close-up of the girl playing a stroke.

The boy returns the shot.

She hits it back and the boy in the foreground starts to run backwards to return it.

In close-up, the boy steps back a bit more and returns the ball with a smash.

Camera pans down as the girl stretches out to return it.

The girl runs backwards, grinning. She has won a point.

The other students watch the exciting rally, waving and cheering, but still without making a sound.

We see the game from THOMAS's end of the court. He stands watching at the corner, leaning on the netting. Suddenly the boy hits the ball so hard it goes right over the back netting and ends up on the grass outside. The girl runs to the back of the court and she and THOMAS unconsciously raise their eyes and follow the flight of the ball.

Camera follows the imaginary arc of the ball as it hits the grass outside the court, rolls a little across the blank, empty green, and then stops.

The girl looks at THOMAS imploringly, begging him with her expression to go and pick up the ball. As he hesitates and seems a little perplexed, she encourages him further by waving and gesturing with her hands. At the far end of the court all the other students stand watching as he moves off, slowly at first.

The students look towards him expectantly, all leaning away from the netting and holding on with one hand.

THOMAS runs towards the point where everyone saw the non-existent ball hit the grass, some way away from the court. He drops his camera and bends down.

THOMAS picks up the imaginary ball, tosses it up and down in his hand two or three times, and then runs forward and hurls it back into the tennis court, watching its path through the air with his eyes.

Then he stands watching the game again, his head moving imperceptibly in time with the movements of the ball. He smiles again, ever so slightly. He is earnest, inscrutable, concentrating on something which is not there. He is very pale. Really not so very different from the white-faced strangers in the park. And very slowly the shots themselves begin to be heard, above the rustling of the wind in the leaves, until they can be recognized as the typical sounds of a tennis ball hitting racquet strings. One on this side, one on that side, one on this side, one on that side. Toc, toc. Toc, toc.

As the sounds become clear, THOMAS lowers his eyes.

Seen from high above, THOMAS is a tiny, solitary figure, standing in a huge expanse of grass. He is serious, worried. He turns towards the right, then turns away and picks up his camera, glancing back in the direction of the tennis court. Then he turns and faces it again. (Still on page 84) Music comes in over. But actually he is not looking at anything. His eyes belong to someone who is following his own thoughts and is not sure if they are anguished or encouraging. THOMAS is erased from the scene and the titles THE END and then BLOW-UP are superimposed on the green expanse of the field.

NOTES

(These notes chiefly describe the differences between the original screenplay and the final version now available for viewing.)

1. The original script began with the following scenes:
   ' It is early morning in London. The iron skeleton of a skyscraper under construction.
   In an old forge used as a studio, a sculptor solders a tube to a sheet of metal.
   Chelsea Art School: a girl stares out of the window, lost in thought. She is standing in front of some of her unfinished paintings: brightly coloured circles. On the other side of a partition, a young man is painstakingly covering a canvas with tiny converging stripes. In another hall a group of art students — teenage boys and girls — are busy drawing two naked women, both of them hideous.
   A school for models. Girls rhythmically roam about the room, drilled by their tutor.
   A rag: students in bizarre clothes and with white powdered faces making a collection in the street.
   A horde of hurrying people surges out of an Underground station dressed in widely differing ways: some of the women are in curious garments, years out of date, others — in very short skirts.
   Long-haired boys stroll in front of Carnaby Street shop windows.
   Young men of the smart set are playing polo in a sunlit park.
   Another park: it is raining on the swans gliding over a lake.
   A third park: wind-swayed branches. A couple of lovers roll on the grass.
   Bill — a slender young artist in his early thirties, wearing a pale blue shirt and white trousers — is unrolling a large sheet of paper across the floor of his studio. He pins it to the floorboards with a special gadget. His wife, Patricia, is in the kitchen making coffee. She pours the coffee and carries it towards Bill. She is a young woman, hiding under her calm appearance, a passionate nature, firmly controlled. As she approaches her husband, she puts down the cup and then turns to look at the sheet of white paper stretched out on the floor, as though she were seeing something drawn on it which is, in fact, not there.
   People at work in some offices — all is calm, quiet, orderly.
   A bedroom in a state of wild disorder. Jane, a strikingly beautiful young woman, is getting out of bed. She sways over to a casual table and switches on the record player. Deafening pop music fills the room.
   The bleak courtyard of a Salvation Army hostel. A small crowd of ragged down-and-outs is emerging from the main gate: old, young, all ages. Among them is Thomas; he is a young man in his late twenties, dishevelled, unshaven for at least a fortnight. As he moves away from the derelict group, he turns round the corner, reaches a blind alley, and climbs into a shining Aston Martin and drives off in true Silverstone style.
   A Pop Group is rehearsing in a bare room. Now and then they break off to work out some new gimmick: a gesture or a yell or something.

Jane comes out into the street and gets into a car beside a distinguished elderly man. The car drives off. Another car follows it, driven by a man of about thirty: his face is tense and hard.

The City is deserted because it is Saturday morning. Thomas's Aston Martin roars along the empty streets.

The Stock Exchange is deserted and looks spotless, like a cathedral.

Smithfield Market. Not much movement. But still an impressive sight.

The slaughterhouse. Empty. But in the side-rails hundreds of head of cattle and horses.

A commercial photographer arranging various food-packets over a lawn, as though composing a still life.

People's faces conveying a whole gamut of feelings — all lively.

Legs, a regiment of legs — all in short skirts.

Models in a street, posing for another photographer.

A group of scantily dressed models posing in a studio.

Another group: pop singers autographing records in a West End store. Here, too, the music is deafening.

Mauve garbage bags in front of smart houses in some Belgravia mews.

Coloured clothes in shop windows along the King's Road and Carnaby Street.

A Rolls-Royce with a woman much too bedecked in jewels, laughing.

The car with Jane and the elderly gentleman is a dark green Alvis. It is still trailed by the other car, a gun-metal Rover. The eyes of its driver are glued to the Alvis. Jane appears to be glancing occasionally at the mirror as if to see whether the Rover is following them. The elderly man driving the Alvis looks positively pleased to have such a lovely young girl at his side.'

2. In the original script there is a different ending to this scene:
'The noise of an engine makes her turn. In the background a car (the gun-metal Rover), appearing out of nowhere, moves towards some bushes. Jane seems annoyed and starts running towards the car.

She stops near some bushes and stands there for a few moments, motionless. Then hurries into the Rover, which makes a U-turn and disappears.

Thomas takes a few more shots of the deserted lawn, then walks away.'

3. The original script had the following:
'The man turns a corner and walks towards the gun-metal Rover, in which we can clearly see Jane sitting at the wheel.'

4. The original script had the following:
'He comes up to the car, gets in, speeds away.

Braking abruptly, the Aston Martin stops in front of the studio door.

Thomas jumps out of the car. Remains a moment beside the telephone booth, lost in thought. Then he enters the studio.'

5. In the original script the following scene occurred before telephoning Ron:
'Thomas picks up one of the innumerable cameras, checks that it's loaded. It isn't.

Thomas returns to the studio. Hunts in a cupboard. Finds at last some new reels and loads the camera hurriedly. He is on the point of going out, but changes his mind.'

6. The original script had the following :
    ' The Aston Martin moves at a moderate speed through a street in central
    London.
    Thomas seems to be examining carefully the fronts of the buildings at shop
    level as if searching for someone or something.
    Then he changes his mind. Steps on the accelerator. Sinks into a tunnel.
    The Aston Martin emerges from the tunnel.
    We are in another street of central London. Very little traffic.
    Thomas slows down again and once again surveys the fronts of the buildings
    on the far side.
    He brings the car to a standstill near the kerb. Jumps out and goes up to
    an automatic machine fixed against the wall. Puts some money into the
    slot, pulls the drawer and takes out a reel of film.
    He goes back to the car and, while loading his camera, looks at the brightly-
    lit shop windows. Suddenly he starts.'

115